HUMMUS
& MORE

CHRISTIAN MOUYSSET
& RONEN GIVON

Photography by

Karen Thomas

METRO BOOKS
New York

RECIPES INSPIRED BY THE **ANCIENT** MEDITERRANEAN, SERVED **WITHOUT** CEREMONY —CUTLERY OPTIONAL

CONTENTS

HUMMUS FOR THE PEOPLE

HUMMUS BROS. WAS BORN ON A GLORIOUS HOT DAY IN MAY 2003, WHEN, AS TWO COLLEGE FRIENDS, WE WERE SEARCHING FOR SOMETHING FILLING AND HEALTHY THAT WOULD TASTE GREAT, AND STILL LEAVE SOME CHANGE FOR DRINKS AT THE UNION BAR.
Passing on the usual options of pizza or sandwiches, we stumbled out of a small delicatessen with three basic ingredients: pita bread, hummus, and olive oil. In no time at all, the bowls of hummus were wiped spotlessly clean. "I could eat a good meal like that every day!," someone remarked. We looked at each other and smiled—a dream was born, to open a place dedicated to hummus.

Having our own place, where hummus could be served and celebrated with imaginative flair, was our one overriding ambition from that day on. We spent every spare moment in our small kitchen— cooking, mixing, and caressing chickpeas to get that perfect combination of texture and taste. Weekends or weekdays, before or after lectures—we just had to get it right. Little did we know how challenging it would be, but after months of experimenting with different ingredients, countless tasting sessions, and facing public scrutiny in busy markets, we finally got there. The recipe was a winner.

Now it was time to take Hummus Bros. to the people.

THE FIRST HUMMUS BROS.

TWO YEARS LATER, IN AUGUST 2005, THE FIRST HUMMUS BROS. OPENED ON WARDOUR STREET IN SOHO, LONDON. IT RECEIVED CRITICAL ACCLAIM AND WE OPENED A SECOND BRANCH IN HOLBORN IN JANUARY 2007. WE NOW RUN FOUR POPULAR BRANCHES ACROSS LONDON.

Our superior-tasting hummus is made daily from carefully selected, fresh ingredients. We serve it with mouth-watering toppings and wonderfully warm pita bread. A unique selection of salads, soups, desserts, and coffee complements the feast.

Inspired taste, value for money, and quality of service is how sophisticated marketing people might describe our offer, but for us, it's simpler than that; it's about making great hummus.

Now, we want to bring it into your home through this book. You will find recipes that the whole family can enjoy—from children (the simple garlic-free hummus is often a winner) to adults, and from meat eaters to vegans. This book is for everyone who wants to eat healthy, filling, and delicious food that is easy to make (we don't do complicated food).

Hummus can be eaten as a dip, main course, or side dish. So whether you are looking to make a hearty dish for a cold winter evening (try Hummus with Chunky Beef (see p. 35), for example), make a salad for a picnic (the Tabbouleh on p. 86 is yummy and zingy), or a light snack/dip (our Basic Hummus (see p. 19) or Falafel (see p. 56 are great for this), we hope you will find a recipe for the occasion.

ABOUT US

8

CONTRARY TO POPULAR BELIEF, WE ARE NOT BROTHERS. HERE'S SOME INFO ABOUT US TO HELP
YOU UNDERSTAND OUR LOVE AFFAIR WITH CHICKPEAS.

RONEN

I was born and raised in Israel on a kibbutz. I used
to hate the food that was served to everyone in
the large communal dining hall and subsequently
was a very fussy eater until my teens. However,
from around the age of 16, hummus became my
obsession—a food to eat with friends on Saturday
afternoons and after evenings out (I still associate
it with that 2 a.m. feeling: plastic furniture on
the sidewalks of Tel Aviv, cars driving past and
honking). This was our fast food; we didn't eat
burgers. It was cheap and accessible.

We used to sit in different hummus places in
Tel Aviv and discuss which one was cleaner, tastier,
grainier, came with better falafel, and which owner
was opening which shop and which one was fatter
because he ate too much bread. We followed the rise
and fall of each place as if it were our own, curious
when a new shop opened up (because the chef from
the guy across the street left and opened his own
place), and sad to see a good place closing because
the guy emigrated to Australia. Each one of my
friends had their preferred hummus restaurant
and frowned upon others' choices (if the meet up
was scheduled in a place that was not my favorite,
I used to complain).

It was as much about the atmosphere that came
with the hummus as the food itself that made a
place worthy of a visit. To this day, it has a social
meaning for me. It's food to share with friends, to
laugh over and love.

The hummus commonly sold in supermarkets
has developed out of Cypriot/Turkish origins, and
became popular in the 1970s. I prefer the Lebanese/
Israeli type, of course, which is smoother and uses
less garlic (if at all), but that's because of where
I come from. Hummus is a sensitive product and
deteriorates in quality quickly if freshly made, so
supermarket stuff is full of preservatives to give it
a longer shelf life. It is healthier to make your
own and it will taste so much better, but making
hummus takes some practice—it won't come out
right the first time, so be ready for that.

For me, the best meal of the week is weekend
brunch—I make Shakshuka (see p. 48) for the
whole family and my friends with a host of other
dishes (which are all found in this book). I get up
early with my daughter and we cook for three
hours. Shakshuka is such a social dish. Try putting
a pot of hummus on the table when you make it
and you will see it's really a match made in heaven.
All my friends keep wanting to be invited over
to enjoy it.

Hummus is such simple dish and so easy to
fall in love with. It's colorful and fresh and so
unassuming. You can bastardize it as you want—
we do! If anyone in the Middle East heard that
we serve hummus with guacamole, they'd think
it was criminal. I'm sure there will be a debate by
the hardcore hummus consumers about what we
do/don't do right, but mainly we want people to look
at our food and say: "I wanna make that."

CHRISTIAN

I am half French/half English. When my family comes together at weekends, we eat my mother's or grandmother's cooking, which will often be Mediterranean-inspired dishes, such as tabouleh, spaghetti Bolognese, salade Niçoise ... and it inspired my love of food from all over the world.

I hadn't eaten hummus at all until I went to university, when I started eating hummus with whatever else was in the refrigerator and soon realized that it could go with anything. The food we serve at Hummus Bros. is predominantly from the Levantine region with an element of this fusion; we serve our hummus with dishes from Mexico, India, Thailand.

We're not accomplished chefs—we don't have a big experimental kitchen. If we taste something good, we try to re-create it as simply as possible, so that it's easy for our chefs to make and always get right. Hopefully this will encourage you to try some of these recipes from two people who knew next to nothing about food or restaurants just nine years ago and who now serve thousands of people daily.

Among my favorite recipes are Hummus with Chunky Beef (see p. 35)—the beef is slow cooked so it is very tender and goes beautifully with the hummus—and the Falafel Salad (see p. 89) with the crunchy cabbage, tzatziki, tomato salsa, and our crispy falafel are also winners (see pp. 56—62). The bread you use to scoop up your hummus is also important. I urge you to try our Whole Weat Pita Bread for this (see p. 110)—it will transform the way you look at hummus for ever.

THE LEVANTINE KITCHEN

THE TERM "LEVANT" FIRST APPEARED IN ENGLISH IN 1497, AND
ORIGINALLY MEANT THE EAST IN GENERAL OR "MEDITERRANEAN
LANDS EAST OF ITALY." IT IS BORROWED FROM THE FRENCH
LEVANT, OR "RISING," THAT IS, THE PLACE WHERE THE SUN RISES.
AT A TIME WHEN THE MEDITERRANEAN WAS THE CENTER OF
THE KNOWN WORLD, THE LEVANT REFERRED TO THE EASTERN
MEDITERRANEAN, LITERALLY, WHERE THE SUN ROSE.

As a geographic and cultural region, the Levant consists of the "eastern
Mediterranean littoral between Anatolia and Egypt" and can be said to
encompass Cyprus, Lebanon, Syria, the Palestinian territories, Jordan,
Israel, part of southern Turkey, and the Aleppo Vilayet.

Perhaps the most distinctive aspects of Levantine cuisine are mezze
dishes, including hummus, tabouleh, falafel, and baba ghanoush.
Chickpeas and tahini (a paste of crushed sesame seeds) feature
heavily. But the nature of the area and its significance as a meeting
point of trading routes, means that flavors from all over the world have
often come together in its food.

Our Levantine style of hummus is smooth and not flavored with
garlic at all. This means it can accept other strong flavors well. Given
how versatile hummus is, we have expanded on this cuisine to include
many dishes from various countries and cultures, such as chicken
tikka or lamb rogan josh from India, guacamole from Mexico, and
a sausage casserole from Eastern Europe.

Our food is nothing new—it's been done before a million times—
but we simplify it to the bare minimum to extract clear, fresh flavors.
The tabouleh is lemony, the fava is earthy, and the hummus is smooth
and very addictive.

12 INGREDIENTS

WHAT ATTRACTED US TO HUMMUS WHEN WE WERE AT COLLEGE WAS HOW EASY IT IS TO MAKE AND EAT WITH WHATEVER FOOD YOU ARE HAVING. JUST SOME CHICKPEAS, A SPOONFUL OF TAHINI, LEMON JUICE, A PINCH OF SALT, AND YOU HAVE THE MAKINGS OF LUNCH. IT IS HEALTHY AND FILLING, AND VEGETARIANS, VEGANS, AND MEAT EATERS, AS WELL AS MOST PEOPLE WITH FOOD INTOLERANCES, CAN ALL EAT IT.

THE CHICKPEA HAS GOOD-NATUREDLY ABSORBED ALMOST EVERY FOOD FAD THAT'S GRIPPED THE NATION OVER THE LAST DECADE, BUT DESPITE ITS POPULARITY, FEW PEOPLE ACTUALLY MAKE THEIR OWN HUMMUS. THIS IS A SHAME, BECAUSE FRESH HUMMUS IS A WORLD AWAY FROM THE SUPERMARKET SOUR SLURRY, SEASONED WITH PRESERVATIVES, AND SOLID ENOUGH TO RETILE THE BATHROOM, AND HALF THE PRICE, TOO. MAKE IT WITH TOP-NOTCH FRESH INGREDIENTS AND IT WILL BLOW YOU AWAY.

CHICKPEAS IN OUR TIME: CANNED VS. DRIED

At Hummus Bros. we make hummus from dried chickpeas that we soak for 12 hours before cooking them. If you are in a rush, you can use canned chickpeas, although we don't recommend it. The dried chickpeas definitely have a nuttier flavor, and they also give the hummus a grainier texture. Many brands of canned chickpeas are crunchy and undercooked; however, you can now buy jars of excellent cooked chickpeas, preserved in water and salt, without added artificial preservatives.

SECRET (SOFTENING) AGENTS

We cook our chickpeas with baking soda to make sure that they are soft enough to make creamy hummus. This prevents the calcium in our London tap water from cementing together the pectin molecules in the pea's cell walls—in fact, the alkaline water that it produces actively encourages these pectins to separate, creating a softening effect.

We use 2 teaspoons (¼oz/10g) of baking soda per 2½ cups (1lb 2oz/500g) of dried chickpeas. After a 12-hour soaking period, the chickpeas take one-quarter of the time to cook and achieve a lovely fluffy texture.

Too much baking soda can give the chickpeas an unpleasant soapy quality, so always err on the side of caution. This also robs them of much of their nutritional value.

THE SKIN OF THE CHICKPEAS

Most people are surprised to find out that chickpeas have a skin. During our research into making the best hummus, we were often told that peeling chickpeas gave a superior color and flavor to the end product. The skin is actually easy to remove once the chickpeas are cooked; however, given the size of the things, it's a tough task. In our experiments, we felt that it was better to keep the skins on and add them, along with the water in which the chickpeas were cooked, to make the hummus "mother" recipe (see p. 19).

OLIVE OIL

Customers often ask if we use olive oil in our hummus. The only oil we use is tahini, which is made from crushed sesame seeds (see below). We do add a drizzle of olive oil to chickpea and fava bean toppings, but none in the hummus itself.

TAHINI

Tahini is the very essence of the flavors of the Levantine kitchen, and the basis for tahini sauce and hummus (it's too thick to eat on its own). The word "tahini" comes from the Hebrew/Arabic root of the word "to grind." It is made from 100 percent sesame seeds, sometimes with a small amount of salt added (typically 0.4 percent in our tahini).

The sesame seeds are cleaned, hulled, and roasted, then ground several times to make the paste we know as tahini.

Different colors of tahini originate either from the type of seed used, or, more often, from the level of roasting. Naturally, the longer the seeds are roasted, the darker the tahini. If the tahini is particularly white, it is possible that the manufacturer used a chemical hulling process with caustic soda, which bleaches the seeds somewhat. It might look good, but it isn't great in terms of nutrition. Some tahini manufacturers have recently started making "whole tahini," which involves hulling, roasting the seeds, and then adding the shells to the mixture which is ground (the shells are not roasted). This results in tahini with a higher calcium content. However, most tahini used in hummus today does not contain the shells.

Look for tahini made with organic "Humera" sesame seeds, usually grown in Ethiopia, and sometimes Paraguay. Some inferior tahini is made from Nigerian seeds, but we only buy tahini with Humera seeds for our restaurant.

Our tahini is not particularly white or dark; it is hulled and tastes slightly salty and almost sweet. It is also particularly thick, whereas a lot of the tahini sold on the market is watery. The ultimate test for tahini is to taste it pure, without any addition of water. If there is an aftertaste (which is usually bitter), then this will certainly come out in the taste of the finished hummus. When you have high-quality tahini made from the right seeds, there is no aftertaste and the consistency is almost like quicksand and sticks to the top of your mouth. If you can easily eat a spoonful of raw tahini, that means it's not good enough.

GARLIC?

The balance of garlic and lemon juice is personal, and this is why in the restaurant we let customers add as much or as little as they want by putting it on the tables as a condiment. We feel that hummus should taste of chickpeas and tahini.

HOW TO TOP IT

Hummus is, of course, an ideal dipping food, but it can be dressed up into a proper meal. Over the years, we have experimented with the best toppings, from traditional boiled chickpeas or fava beans with a hard-boiled egg to vegetarian toppings, such as Mixed Vegetable Salad (see p. 88) or Falafel Salad (see p. 89), and meat toppings, such as Chunky Beef (see p. 35) or Lamb Rogan Josh (see p. 38).

HEALTHY HUMMUS

1 HEALTH BENEFITS OF CHICKPEAS
Chickpeas are particularly healthy because they do not contain any cholesterol or saturated fats but are rich in protein. This makes hummus a favorite among vegetarians. A fantastic source of slow-release energy, chickpeas are also known to be effective in preventing the buildup of cholesterol in blood vessels and can help maintain correct blood sugar levels.

2 NUTRITIONAL VALUE OF TAHINI
Tahini, meanwhile, is full of fat and calories. However, the fact that it is used sparingly in most hummus recipes and that it mostly contains unsaturated fat means there is not much to worry about. Tahini is also high in protein and is a great source of valuable calcium.

**3 OPTIONAL ADDITIONS:
GARLIC, LEMON JUICE, OLIVE OIL**
Another healthy ingredient often found alongside hummus is olive oil. As most people know, olive oil is a healthy fat, because it has a high monounsaturated fat content but is low in saturated fat. This oil can help regulate cholesterol and protect the heart from various diseases. Garlic and lemon juice, meanwhile, are filled with antioxidants that reduce oxidative stress in the body. They also work to improve immune functions and the fight of bacteria and viruses. And, of course, lemon juice is full of vitamin C.

4 GENERAL HEALTH BENEFITS OF HUMMUS
Hummus as a whole contains plenty of omega-3 fatty acids, which are great for improving intelligence and maintaining a healthy heart. On top of it all, this dish also has iron, vitamin B_6, manganese, copper, folic acid, and amino acids. Tryptophan, phenylalanine, and tyrosine are the amino acids found in hummus that can promote good-quality sleep and uplift one's mood.

HUMMUS IS LOADED WITH NUTRIENTS THAT CAN CONTRIBUTE TO A HEALTHY LIFESTYLE. INCLUDE IT IN YOUR DIET BY USING IT AS A SPREAD ON SANDWICHES AND WRAPS, AS A BASE FOR YOUR SALAD, AS A DIP FOR RAW VEGETABLES, OR AS A SIDE DISH FOR MAIN DISHES.

MAKING
HUMMUS

BASIC HUMMUS RECIPE

SERVES: 16–20
MAKES: ABOUT 11 CUPS
(4LB/1.8KG)
PREP: 15 MINUTES
SOAK: 12 HOURS,
OR OVERNIGHT
COOK: 1–1½ HOURS

DON'T BE DECEIVED. ALTHOUGH THE SIMPLEST OF PROCESSES, MAKING HUMMUS IS AN ART FORM. IT TAKES PRACTICE TO GET IT JUST RIGHT, BUT ONCE YOU, DO THE REWARDS ARE HUGE.

OK, SO YOU NEED TO REMEMBER TO SOAK THE CHICKPEAS THE DAY BEFORE, BUT THERE REALLY IS LITTLE INVOLVED WITH SOAKING OR COOKING THEM.

ALL THE INGREDIENTS ARE RELATIVELY INEXPENSIVE, HOWEVER, DO TRY TO FIND THE BEST TAHINI (SESAME PASTE), BECAUSE YOUR HUMMUS WILL TASTE SO MUCH BETTER.

THE FOLLOWING RECIPE IS FOR A LARGE QUANTITY, BUT IT STORES WELL FOR UP TO THREE DAYS IN THE REFRIGERATOR AND IT'S QUICKLY EATEN BY THE AVERAGE HOUSEHOLD. IF YOU PREFER, THE RECIPE IS EASILY HALVED.

SEE THE FOLLOWING PAGES FOR THE METHOD.

20

1 Put the chickpeas into a bowl and cover with plenty of cold water (they will expand as they soak). Cover and let soak—there's no need to refrigerate them—for 12 hours or overnight. There aren't any shortcuts to this; just aim to put them to soak the day before you need them.

2 Drain the chickpeas and put into a medium saucepan. Pour in the fresh measured cold water so that the water covers the chickpeas by only about ¾ inch (2cm). Stir in the baking soda, then bring the water to a boil. Don't be tempted to add salt at this stage, because it can make the chickpeas tough. Keep a watchful eye as it comes to the boil—it can easily boil over.

3 Skim off scum, if desired, with a slotted spoon. Cook over medium heat for 1–1½ hours until the chickpeas are soft. If the water level seems to be going down too quickly, partly cover the pan with a lid to help reduce evaporation, but don't cover the top completely or the pan will boil over. Keep an eye on the water level and top up with a little extra boiling water, if needed, especially toward the end of

cooking. Stir from time to time, stirring more toward the end of cooking, as the chickpeas take on a soupy texture because there is less water in the pan.

4 Once cooked, drain the liquid if there is a lot, but don't throw it away—keep it for later to adjust the consistency. Spread the chickpeas over the surface of a large roasting pan and let cool.

5 You should have about 7¾ cups (2lb 7oz/1.25kg) cooked chickpeas. Puree, in batches, with any liquid from the roasting pan in a food processor, adding the tahini, lemon juice, and salt to taste until you have a creamy, velvety smooth consistency. Adjust the consistency with some of the reserved cooking liquid or water. You may need to do this in batches, depending on the size of your machine. Make sure it's nice and thick, but smooth with no lumps.

6 Transfer the hummus to a large plastic container, spread it level, then press on a well-fitting lid. Chill until needed.
.

2½ cups (1lb 2oz/500g) dried chickpeas

5 cups (2 pints/1.2 liters) cold water

2 teaspoons baking soda

scant 1¼ cups (10½oz/300g) tahini

juice of 2 lemons

sea salt, to taste

NOTE

THE COOKING TIME MAY VARY; OLD CHICKPEAS WILL TAKE LONGER TO COOK THAN THIS SEASON'S CROP. YOU'RE AIMING FOR ESPECIALLY SOFT CHICKPEAS; IT DOESN'T MATTER IF THEY BREAK UP BECAUSE THEY WILL BE PROCESSED ANYWAY. IF IN DOUBT, SIMPLY SCOOP OUT A FEW CHICKPEAS, THROW THEM AT THE WALL, AND IF THEY STICK, THEY'RE READY.

22 HOW TO ACHIEVE THE PERFECT HUMMUS BROS. SWIRL

1 Plop a large mound of hummus onto your chosen plate—a shallow bowl is the ideal thing.

2 Choose a large spoon with a round bottom—a tablespoon or large soup spoon will be perfect for the job.

3 Place the spoon, bowl-side down, in the center of the mound and rock it back and forth until you have created a bowl-shape cavity.

4 Pressing firmly, continue to enlarge the bowl, pressing the hummus out to the sides of your plate.

5 As you go around, push the spoon slightly under the rim of hummus—it takes practice, but you want perfection, right? This is also a test of your hummus' consistency. If you made it too watery, the crater you just created will collapse into the center of the bowl.

6 Then, turn the spoon over onto its edge and carefully scrape it around the edge of the hummus until the sides are nice and smooth.

7 Now you're ready to fill it with whatever you feel like. Your friends will think your presentation skills are outstanding, and you can rightfully bask in the glow of adulation.

TOPPINGS FOR HUMMUS

26

HUMMUS WITH SLOW-COOKED CHICKPEAS

1⅓ cups (9oz/250g) dried chickpeas, soaked overnight in plenty of cold water

scant 3 cups (1¼ pints/700ml) cold water

1 tablespoon olive oil

1 tablespoon ground cumin seeds

To finish:

2 cups (1lb/450g) Hummus (see p. 19)

3 tablespoons olive oil

juice of 1 lemon

tahini sauce

sea salt

paprika, to taste

chopped fresh flat-leaf parsley, for sprinkling

THIS IS A DOUBLE WHAMMY OF CHICKPEAS, FULL OF TASTE, NOT TO MENTION FIBER, PROTEIN, AND HEALTHY SLOW-RELEASE CARBS TO POWER YOU THROUGH THE AFTERNOON.

1 Drain the soaked chickpeas, put into a medium saucepan, and pour in the water so that the chickpeas are covered by about ¾ inch (2cm). Add the oil and cumin and bring to a boil. Skim off any scum, if desired, then partly cover with a lid and cook over medium heat for 40–60 minutes until the chickpeas are tender but still a good shape. Drain in a strainer set over a bowl to catch the cooking liquid.

2 Spread the Hummus over four serving plates and make a small well in the middle. Add a few spoonfuls of chickpeas to each well. Dress each portion with plenty of olive oil, lemon juice, and tahini sauce, then season to taste. Moisten with some of the reserved cooking liquid, if necessary, and top with a little paprika and chopped parsley.

TIP

QUARTER A WHITE ONION AND SOAK IN A BOWL OF WATER FOR 30 MINUTES. DRAIN AND PEEL OFF THE INDIVIDUAL LAYERS, THEN USE TO SCOOP UP THE HUMMUS AND CHICKPEAS.

SERVES 4
PREP: 10 MINUTES
COOK:
17–18 MINUTES

2 tablespoons olive oil

1 onion, finely diced

1 leek, thinly sliced, keeping white
and green slices separated

3 scallions, thinly sliced

2–3 garlic cloves, finely chopped

1 (14½-oz/400-g) can diced tomatoes

small handful each of fresh basil,
parsley, and oregano, coarsely
chopped, plus extra to garnish

2–3 fresh thyme sprigs, leaves only

sea salt and freshly ground
black pepper

14oz (400g) white button mushrooms,
wiped clean and left whole

To serve:

2 cups (1lb/450g) Hummus
(see p. 19)

paprika, to taste

tahini (optional)

1 small onion, quartered, soaked, and
layers separated (see p. 26)

HUMMUS WITH MUSHROOMS

A RICH, GARLICKY TOMATO SAUCE SPECKLED WITH THREE
DIFFERENT HERBS COVERS THESE DELICIOUS MUSHROOMS.
BASIL, PARSLEY, AND OREGANO WORK WELL TOGETHER, BUT
YOU CAN MIX AND MATCH THE HERBS, DEPENDING ON WHAT
YOU HAVE IN THE REFRIGERATOR OR GROWING IN A FLOWERPOT
ON THE WINDOWSILL. FRESH OREGANO CAN BE DIFFICULT TO
FIND, SO USE 1 TEASPOON DRIED IF YOU CAN'T GET HOLD OF IT.

1 Heat the oil in a large skillet, add the onion and white sliced leeks, and sauté gently for 5 minutes, stirring from time to time, until softened and just beginning to turn golden around the edges.

2 Add the green sliced leeks, scallions, and garlic and sauté for 1–2 minutes. Mix in the tomatoes, chopped herbs, and thyme leaves. Season well with salt and black pepper and then bring to a boil.

3 Add the mushrooms, lower the heat, cover with a lid, and simmer gently for 10 minutes, stirring from time to time until the mushrooms are just cooked. It will become more watery as the mushrooms cook and release their juices.

4 Spoon onto serving plates spread with Hummus, garnish with a few extra chopped herbs, and serve with a spoonful of yogurt on the side sprinkled with a little paprika, with tahini (if using), and serve with pieces of onion to scoop up the mushroom mixture.

SERVES 4
PREP: 15 MINUTES
COOK: 1 HOUR
25 MINUTES

HUMMUS WITH CHICKEN

2 tablespoons olive oil

1¼lb (600g) skinless, boneless chicken thigh meat, cubed

1 onion, coarsely chopped

2 garlic cloves, finely chopped

2 teaspoons sweet mild paprika

2 teaspoons ground cumin

1 teaspoon ground coriander

1 (14½-oz/400-g) can diced tomatoes

sea salt and freshly ground black pepper

small handful of fresh flat-leaf parsley, coarsely chopped

2 cups (1lb/450g) Hummus (see p. 19), to serve

THIS IS SO EASY TO MAKE FOR A FAMILY SUPPER OR FOR FRIENDS TO SHARE. SUCCULENT CHICKEN, LIGHTLY FRIED IN OLIVE OIL WITH GARLIC, PAPRIKA, AND OUR FAVORITE SPICES, CUMIN AND CORIANDER, THEN TOPPED WITH FRESH TASTING PARSLEY. CHEAT AND USE ALREADY BONED AND SKINNED CHICKEN THIGHS OR BREASTS, IF YOU PREFER.

1 Heat 1 tablespoon of the oil in a large skillet, add a few pieces of chicken at a time to the hot oil, then gradually add the rest until it's all in the pan. Cook over medium heat for about 5 minutes, stirring from time to time, until golden brown, then scoop the chicken out of the pan with a slotted spoon and transfer to a plate.

2 Add the remaining oil to the skillet, then sauté the onion for 5 minutes until softened and just beginning to turn golden brown. Stir in the garlic, paprika, cumin, and ground coriander and cook for 1 minute, then return the chicken to the pan and coat in the spices.

3 Pour in the tomatoes and season well with salt and black pepper. Bring to a boil, then lower the heat to the lowest possible point and simmer for 1¼ hours, or until the chicken is cooked through with no hint of pink juices (a heat diffuser can help here).

4 When ready to serve, stir most of the chopped parsley into the chicken, then spoon onto serving plates spread with Hummus and sprinkle with the remaining parsley.

HUMMUS WITH CHUNKY BEEF

2 tablespoons olive oil

1½lb (650g) lean diced stewing beef, such as chuck steak

1 onion, chopped

1 teaspoon ground coriander

1 teaspoon ground cumin

2 teaspoons sweet mild paprika

1 (14½-oz/400-g) can diced tomatoes

1¼ cups (10fl oz/300ml) beef stock or broth

small handful of fresh cilantro, coarsely chopped, plus extra to garnish

small handful of fresh parsley, coarsely chopped, plus extra to garnish

large pinch of sea salt

1 teaspoon coarsely ground black pepper

2 cups (1lb/450g) Hummus (see p. 19), to serve

plain yogurt or Tzatziki (see p. 102), to serve

GIVE AN EVERYDAY BEEF CASSEROLE A LEVANTINE-STYLE TWIST WITH OUR FAVORITE GROUND SPICES, CUMIN AND CORIANDER, PLUS SOME CHOPPED FRESH PARSLEY, TOO. THIS WILL KEEP WELL IN THE REFRIGERATOR FOR UP TO 3 DAYS.

1 Heat 1 tablespoon of the oil in a large skillet, add the beef, a few pieces at a time until all the pieces are in the pan, and sauté over medium heat for about 5 minutes, stirring from time to time until browned. Scoop out of the pan with a slotted spoon and set aside.

2 Add the remaining oil to the skillet, then sauté the onion over medium heat for 5 minutes until softened and just beginning to turn golden brown. Stir in the ground spices and cook briefly to release their flavors, then stir in the tomatoes, stock, chopped herbs, salt, and black pepper. Bring to a boil, then return the beef to the pan.

3 Turn the heat as low as it will go (a heat diffuser can help here) and cook for 2½–3 hours, or until the beef is tender, stirring occasionally. Serve spooned onto serving plates spread with Hummus and garnished with extra chopped herbs and a spoonful of yogurt or Tzatziki on the side.

SERVES 4
PREP: 15 MINUTES
COOK:
2 HOURS 40 MINUTES–
3 HOURS 10 MINUTES

36

SERVES 4
PREP: 10 MINUTES
COOK: 45 MINUTES

HUMMUS WITH LAMB & PINE NUTS

1 tablespoon olive oil

1 large red onion, finely chopped

1lb (450g) ground lamb

2 tablespoons (1oz/25g) butter

scant 2 cups (16fl oz/450ml) lamb stock or broth

2/3 cup (3oz/85g) bulgur wheat

2 teaspoons ground cumin

1½ teaspoons ground cinnamon

½ teaspoon chili powder

1 teaspoon granulated sugar

sea salt and freshly ground black pepper

scant 1/3 cup (2oz/55g) pine nuts, toasted

2 cups (1lb/450g) Hummus (see p. 19)

To garnish:

tahini

paprika, to taste

THIS IS THE CLASSIC LEBANESE WAY OF SERVING MEAT WITH HUMMUS. THE CINNAMON-FLAVORED MEAT AND NUTS BLEND PERFECTLY WITH THE HUMMUS, SERVED HERE WITH A LITTLE GREEN CHILI SAUCE (SEE P. 104) ON THE SIDE.

1 Heat the oil in a large skillet, add the onion, and sauté over medium heat for 5 minutes, stirring until just beginning to brown around the edges. Add the lamb and butter and cook, stirring from time to time and breaking up the meat with a wooden spoon, until browned and tender.

2 Meanwhile, bring the stock to a boil in a saucepan, add the bulgur wheat, cover, lower the heat, and simmer for 10 minutes until just tender with just enough stock left to keep the bulgur wheat moist.

3 Add the cumin, cinnamon, and chili powder to the meat, then stir in the sugar and season with salt and black pepper. Cover with a lid and cook for 10 minutes. Add the bulgur and stock to the meat, then add about two-thirds of the pine nuts. Stir together, cover, and cook gently for 10 minutes.

4 Spoon onto serving plates spread with Hummus, then sprinkle with the rest of the pine nuts. Add a spoonful of tahini, sprinkle with a little paprika to garnish, and serve.

HUMMUS WITH LAMB ROGAN JOSH

2 tablespoons olive oil

1 onion, minced (process in a food processor if you have one)

1½lb (650g) boneless shoulder of lamb, cut into large dice

1-inch (2.5-cm) piece fresh ginger, grated

2 garlic cloves, finely chopped

½ teaspoon chili powder

1 teaspoon turmeric

1 teaspoon garam masala

1 teaspoon ground coriander

2 teaspoons ground cumin

¼ teaspoon sea salt

2 tomatoes, diced

⅔ cup (5fl oz/150ml) water

scant ½ cup (3½oz/100g) Greek yogurt

2 cups (1lb/450g) Hummus (see p. 19), to serve

chopped fresh cilantro, to garnish

IT MIGHT SEEM A STRANGE COMBINATION—INDIAN CURRY WITH HUMMUS—BUT OUR CUSTOMERS JUST LOVE IT. ALWAYS BUY SHOULDER OF LAMB IF YOU CAN, BECAUSE THE MEAT HAS A NATURAL SWEETNESS AND JUST MELTS IN THE MOUTH WHEN COOKED THIS WAY, BUT OTHER CUTS OF LAMB CAN WORK WELL, TOO.

1 Heat the oil in a large skillet, add the onion, and sauté over low heat for 3–4 minutes, stirring until softened. Add the lamb, a few pieces at a time, until all the pieces are in the pan. Cook over medium heat for 10 minutes, stirring from time to time, until the lamb is browned.

2 Stir in the ginger and garlic, then mix in the ground spices and salt. Cover with a lid and cook for 20–25 minutes, stirring from time to time, until the spices form a crust around the lamb and the oil has begun to separate slightly.

3 Add the tomatoes and water, replace the lid, and cook for 30 minutes, stirring from time to time, until the lamb is meltingly tender. Remove from the heat and stir in the yogurt.

4 Spoon onto serving plates spread with Hummus and sprinkle with a little chopped cilantro before serving.

SERVES 4
PREP: 20 MINUTES
COOK: I HOUR–
I HOUR 10 MINUTES

HUMMUS WITH CHILI CON CARNE

SERVES 4
PREP: 15 MINUTES
COOK: 1 HOUR
10 MINUTES

1 tablespoon olive oil

1 onion, finely chopped

1lb (450g) lean ground beef, such as ground round or ground sirloin

½ each of red, green, and yellow bell peppers, cored, seeded, and diced

2 garlic cloves, finely chopped

1 carrot, diced

½ teaspoon ground cinnamon

1 teaspoon ground cumin

1 teaspoon chili powder

1 teaspoon coarsely ground black pepper

sea salt

1 (14½-oz/400-g) can diced tomatoes

1 tablespoon granulated sugar

1 (15-oz/425-g) can red kidney beans, rinsed and drained

up to 1¼ cups (10fl oz/300ml) beef stock or broth

To serve:

2 cups (1lb/450g) Hummus (see p. 19)

sour cream

Guacamole (see p. 100)

SERVING THIS FAVORITE ON A BED OF HUMMUS WILL GET YOUR FRIENDS TALKING, BUT THE CREAMY SMOOTHNESS OF THE HUMMUS REALLY WORKS WELL WITH THE MELLOW HEAT OF THE CHILI AND MAKES A CHANGE FROM PLAIN BOILED RICE. IT'S DELICIOUS TOPPED WITH SOUR CREAM AND GUACAMOLE, OR, IF YOU PREFER YOUR FOOD EXTRA HOT, TRY THIS TOPPED WITH A SPOONFUL OF GREEN CHILI SAUCE (SEE P. 104).

1 Heat the oil in a large saucepan, add the onion, and sauté over medium heat for 5 minutes, stirring from time to time, until softened and just beginning to turn golden. Stir in the beef and cook for 20 minutes, stirring and breaking up the meat with a wooden spoon, until browned and tender.

2 Stir in the diced bell peppers, garlic, and carrot and cook for a few minutes to soften. Stir in the ground spices, black pepper, and sea salt and cook for another 1–2 minutes to bring out all the flavors.

3 Mix in the tomatoes, sugar, drained kidney beans, and stock. Bring to a boil, then cover with a lid, lower the heat to low, and cook for 40 minutes, stirring from time to time.

4 Spoon onto serving plates spread with Hummus, then top with spoonfuls of sour cream and Guacamole.

40

1 tablespoon olive oil

1 onion, chopped

1lb (450g) ground beef, such as
ground round or ground sirloin

2 garlic cloves, finely chopped

2 teaspoons sweet mild paprika

1 teaspoon ground cumin

1 teaspoon ground coriander

½ teaspoon chili powder

1 teaspoon granulated sugar

sea salt and freshly ground
black pepper

1¼ cups (10fl oz/300ml)
beef stock or broth

1 tablespoon tomato paste

To serve:

2 cups (1lb/450g) Hummus (see p. 19)

grated cheese

Tomato & Cilantro Salsa (see p. 103)
or Guacamole (see p. 100)

warm Whole Wheat Pita Breads
(see p. 110)

Green Chili Sauce (see p. 104),
(optional)

HUMMUS WITH MEXICAN BEEF

THIS RECIPE IS THE BRAINCHILD OF OUR ORIGINAL MARKETING MANAGER, AN AMERICAN FROM FLORIDA, WHO JUST KNEW THIS COMBINATION WOULD WORK WELL. WE RECENTLY CONDUCTED A SURVEY OF FAVORITE TOPPINGS AND MEXICAN BEEF CAME OUT ON TOP. THANK YOU, RYAN.

1 Heat the oil in a large skillet, add the onion, and sauté over medium heat for 5 minutes, stirring until just beginning to brown around the edges. Add the beef and cook for 20 minutes, stirring and breaking up the meat with a wooden spoon, until browned and tender.

2 Add the garlic, ground spices, and chili powder to the meat, then stir in the sugar and season with salt and black pepper. Cover with a lid and cook for 10 minutes, then mix in the stock and tomato paste. Replace the lid and cook for 10 minutes.

3 Spoon onto serving plates spread with Hummus, then top with grated cheese and spoonfuls of Tomato & Cilantro Salsa or Guacamole. Serve with warm Pita Breads and Green Chili Sauce, if desired.

HUMMUS WITH MOROCCAN MEATBALLS

4 slices of bread (about 4½oz/125g), torn into pieces

1lb (450g) lean ground beef, such as ground round or ground sirloin

2 eggs

1 teaspoon chili powder

½ teaspoon ground cinnamon

sea salt and freshly ground black pepper

2 cups (1lb/450g) Hummus (see p. 19), to serve

fresh parsley or basil leaves, to garnish

For the tomato sauce:

1 tablespoon olive oil

1 onion, finely chopped

2 celery stalks, finely chopped

2–3 garlic cloves, finely chopped

½ teaspoon chili powder

2 (14½-oz/400-g) cans diced tomatoes

2 teaspoons granulated sugar

SERVES 4
PREP: 20 MINUTES
COOK: 30 MINUTES

CHRISTIAN: THIS IS MY FAVORITE TOPPING BY FAR AND IT GOES PARTICULARLY WELL WITH GUACAMOLE. MEATBALLS ARE ALWAYS POPULAR IN THE RESTAURANT, BUT PEOPLE ARE PUT OFF MAKING THEM AT HOME BECAUSE THEY THINK THEY'RE TOO MUCH WORK. IF YOU HAVE A FOOD PROCESSOR, JUST PUT EVERYTHING IN TOGETHER AND PROCESS IN SECONDS. THEN ADD THE MEATBALLS TO OUR EASY TOMATO SAUCE AND LET SIMMER GENTLY WHILE YOU GET ON WITH SOMETHING ELSE.

1 Process the bread in a food processor until fine crumbs form. Add the ground beef and eggs, then spoon in the chili powder and cinnamon. Season generously with salt and black pepper, then process together until well mixed. If you don't have a food processor, make bread crumbs in a blender or rub over a coarse grater, then mix with the remaining ingredients in a bowl.

2 Using a tablespoon, scoop out the meatball mixture on to a cutting board or baking sheet into 24 mounds, then shape into balls by hand.

3 For the sauce, heat the oil in a large, deep skillet with a lid, add the onion and celery, and sauté over low heat for 5 minutes until soft and just beginning to

turn golden. Stir in the garlic and chili powder, then the tomatoes and sugar. Season with salt and black pepper, then cover and simmer gently for 5 minutes.

4 Remove the lid from the pan and add the meatballs in a single layer, if there's room. Cover and cook over low heat for 15 minutes. Uncover, turn the meatballs and cook for another 5 minutes until the sauce has thickened and the meatballs are cooked through. To test if they are cooked, take out one of the meatballs and cut it in half; there should be no hint of pink.

5 Spoon onto serving plates spread with Hummus and top with parsley or basil or a mixture of them both.

MASABACHA

1 quantity of hot Slow-Cooked Chickpeas (see p. 26), with a little of their cooking liquid

2 cups (1lb/450g) Hummus (see p. 19)

1 cup (8oz/225g) plain tahini

To serve:

4–5 tablespoons olive oil

1–2 lemons, juiced or cut into wedges

4 hard-boiled eggs, peeled and quartered

1 teaspoon ground cumin

1 teaspoon sweet mild paprika

large handful of fresh flat-leaf parsley, coarsely torn

2–3 garlic cloves, finely chopped (optional)

warm Whole Wheat Pita Breads (see p. 110) or onion scoops (see p. 26)

NOTES

Always make sure the dish is swimming in plenty of lemon and oil. Put the garlic on the side as an option and let your guests decide if they want it.

Pita bread has a tendency to dry out if not kept properly covered. If you have pita breads that are not 100 percent fresh, sprinkle a tiny amount of water over and put in a warm oven for 2–3 minutes (watch carefully) to revive them.

NOT FOR THE FAINT-HEARTED! MASABACHA IS FOR HUMMUS FANATICS WHO WANT TO TAKE IT TO THE NEXT LEVEL—IT HAS INDULGENCE WRITTEN ALL OVER IT. A MAIN MEAL IN ISRAELI CULTURE, COMMONLY SERVED WARM, IT HAS A UNIQUE COMBINATION OF TEXTURES (CHEWY CHICKPEAS, SMOOTH HUMMUS, STICKY TAHINI). IT'S A HEAVENLY MIXTURE.

WHATEVER YOU ADD HERE, MAKE SURE THERE'S PLENTY OF IT: HUMMUS, TAHINI, LEMON, AND COPIOUS QUANTITIES OF OLIVE OIL. SLICE AN EGG ON TOP (HARD-BOILED FOR 8 HOURS IF YOU'RE A PURIST, ALTHOUGH A 10-MINUTE EGG IS FINE, TOO) AND SPRINKLE WITH COARSELY CHOPPED PARSLEY AND GARLIC (ONLY IF YOU'RE INTO GARLIC—IT'S NOT ESSENTIAL). NOW DIVE IN WITH FRESH PITA OR A SCOOP OF ONION. AND DON'T EXPECT TO GET MUCH WORK DONE AFTER THE FEAST!

1 In a large saucepan, warm the Slow-Cooked Chickpeas with a little of their liquid, then throw in a dollop of Hummus followed by the tahini and gently mix together to warm through. Sprinkle with plenty of olive oil and lemon juice. Don't keep it in the pan long; you need just about 30 seconds to get the Hummus mixing with the Slow-Cooked Chickpeas and warming up. The whole thing should be served at just above room temperature, not hot.

2 Divide the mixture among deep bowls and add the quartered egg. Season to taste with extra lemon juice, olive oil, cumin, and paprika, then top with plenty of parsley. Serve with fresh lemon juice (with finely chopped garlic on the side, if you wish), or for a more visual effect, add a lemon wedge instead of the juice mixture—it adds color. Serve with warm Pita Breads or onion scoops.

SERVES 4
PREP: 15 MINUTES
COOK: 8 MINUTES

1½ cups (9oz/250g) dried split fava beans, soaked overnight in cold water

scant 3 cups (1¼ pints/700ml) cold water

2 tablespoons olive oil

juice of 1 lemon

2 teaspoons ground cumin

sea salt and freshly ground black pepper

To finish:

2 cups (1lb/450g) Hummus (see p. 19)

extra virgin olive oil

small handful of fresh parsley, finely chopped

ground cumin

Green Chili Sauce (see p. 104)

lemon wedges

warm Whole Wheat Pita Breads (see p. 110) or

2 onions, quartered, soaked, and layers separated (see p. 26)

4 hard-boiled eggs (optional)

HUMMUS WITH FAVA BEANS

THE TRADITIONAL WAY OF EATING BREAKFAST HUMMUS, ORIGINATING IN EGYPTIAN CUISINE, MANUAL WORKERS WOULD HAVE THIS FOR BREAKFAST IN ANTICIPATION OF A HARD WORKING DAY AHEAD. FAVA BEANS ARE NOT ALWAYS EASY TO FIND, BUT MAKE THE EFFORT BECAUSE THEY'RE HEALTHY AND THE WHOLE DISH IS JUST SO DISTINCTIVE—NOTHING ELSE TASTES QUITE LIKE IT. SLICE AN EGG ON TOP TO MAKE IT EVEN MORE AUTHENTIC, IF YOU WANT. DRIZZLE WITH PLENTY OF OLIVE OIL, LEMON JUICE, PARSLEY, AND A LITTLE CUMIN, AND LET THE FLAVORS TRANSPORT YOU TO A FAR AWAY LAND.

1 Drain the soaked beans, put into a medium saucepan, and pour in the water so that the beans are covered by about ¾ inch (2cm). Add the olive oil, lemon juice, cumin, and plenty of salt and black pepper, then bring to a boil. Partly cover with a lid and cook over medium heat for 45–60 minutes, or until the beans are soft and mash easily between two fingers.

2 Pour the beans into a colander set above a bowl to catch the cooking liquid, then add half the beans back into the empty pan with a little of the reserved cooking liquid. Grind with an immersion blender, or transfer the beans and liquid to a food processor and process, gradually adding more of the cooking liquid as needed to make a thick, spreadable consistency. If you have been a little heavy-handed with the liquid, add a few more beans. Once you get the texture right, gradually add more beans and a little more cooking liquid until all the beans have been ground. Taste and adjust the seasoning as needed.

3 Spread the Hummus over serving plates, then top with spoonfuls of the warm fava bean mix. Finish with plenty of extra olive oil and chopped parsley and serve with Green Chili Sauce and lemon wedges to squeeze over the top, and warm Pita Breads or pieces of onion to scoop up the bean mix. Slices of hard-boiled egg will complete the dish, but you can omit them if you prefer.

SHAKSHUKA

12 plum tomatoes (about 1lb 10oz/750g)

2 tablespoons olive oil

2 onions, finely chopped

1–1½ large mild red chilis, seeded and finely chopped

3½oz (100g) chorizo sausage, thinly sliced

1 tablespoon tomato paste

1½ teaspoons superfine or granulated sugar

1 teaspoon smoked mild paprika

sea salt and freshly ground black pepper

4–8 eggs

1 teaspoon dried oregano

crusty bread or challah, to serve

IDEAL FOR SATURDAY BRUNCH, THIS IS ONE OF THOSE RECIPES THAT THE MORE YOU MAKE IT, THE BETTER IT WILL BE; ONLY BY MAKING IT 20 TIMES WILL YOU GET PERFECT RESULTS. SERVE ONE OR TWO EGGS PER PORTION, DEPENDING ON HOW HUNGRY YOUR BRUNCH GUESTS ARE. YOU MIGHT WANT TO EXPERIMENT WITH EXTRA INGREDIENTS: MORE CHILI OR MORE CHORIZO, SCALLIONS TO GARNISH, EVEN DICED MOZZARELLA SPRINKLED OVER AT THE END.

1 Make a cross cut in the bottom of each tomato, put into a heatproof bowl, and pour over boiling water to just cover them. Let stand for 1 minute until the skins begin to peel away, then drain and rinse with cold water until cool enough to handle. Peel away the skins with a sharp knife. Chop the tomatoes into ½-inch (1-cm) dice, leaving in the seeds.

2 Heat the oil in a large skillet, add the onions and chilis, and sauté for 2–3 minutes until just beginning to soften. Add the chorizo and cook for another 2–3 minutes until the onion is beginning to brown with the chorizo juices.

SERVES 4
PREP: 15 MINUTES
COOK: 1 HOUR

3 Stir in the tomatoes, tomato paste, and sugar, then add the paprika and salt and black pepper. Cover and cook over low heat for 30 minutes, stirring every 10 minutes or so until the

tomatoes are really soft. Keep a watchful eye as they cook; if the heat is a little high, you may need to stir in a little extra water to stop them from drying out completely.

4 When the mixture is dry (but not burned), uncover and stir the sauce, then, with a large spoon, make little dips or craters large enough to hold the eggs. Try not to position the dips too close to the edge of the pan. If the sauce is a little too runny, simmer over slightly higher heat, stirring, for 5 minutes or so until it has thickened. Carefully break an egg into each dip, being careful not to break the yolks. Sprinkle the oregano and a little extra salt over the yolks, then replace the lid and cook gently for 5–10 minutes until the egg whites are set and the yolks cooked to your preference. You want to poach/steam the eggs instead of fry them. Serve with some crusty bread or challah.

50

SERVES 4
PREP: 15 MINUTES
COOK:
22–28 MINUTES

HUMMUS WITH SPICY SAUSAGE & THREE-PEPPER STEW

2 tablespoons olive oil

1 onion, chopped

1 red bell pepper, halved, cored, seeded, and diced

1 green bell pepper, halved, cored, seeded, and diced

1 yellow bell pepper, halved, cored, seeded, and diced

10½oz (300g) Kabanos Polish sausage, thickly sliced

8 plum tomatoes (about 1lb 2oz/500g), diced (no need to peel)

2 zucchini, diced

2 red chilis, halved, seeded, and finely chopped

sea salt and freshly ground black pepper

1 tablespoon tomato paste

1–2 green chilis, halved, seeded, and finely chopped

2 cups (1lb/450g) Hummus (see p. 19), to serve

PACKED WITH COLORFUL MEDITERRANEAN VEGETABLES, THIS STOVE-TOP STEW IS FLAVORED WITH RED AND GREEN CHILIS. THE AMOUNT YOU USE IS VERY MUCH UP TO YOU. IF YOU PREFER YOUR FOOD HOT AND SPICY, YOU CAN ADJUST THE HEAT AT THE END WHEN ADDING THE GREEN CHILI.

1 Heat the oil in a large, deep skillet with a lid, add the onion and diced bell peppers, and sauté over medium heat for 10–15 minutes, stirring from time to time until the bell peppers are softened.

2 Stir in the sliced Polish sausage, the tomatoes, zucchini, and red chilis. Season generously with salt and black pepper, then cover and cook for 10 minutes, stirring from time to time, until the tomatoes are softened and saucy.

3 Mix in the tomato paste, then gradually add half the green chilis and cook for 2–3 minutes. Taste and adjust with extra chili to taste.

4 Spoon onto serving plates spread with Hummus, then drizzle with the pan juices and serve piping hot.

SERVES 4
PREP: 30 MINUTES
MARINATE: 6 HOURS,
OR OVERNIGHT
COOK: 46 MINUTES–
1 HOUR

HUMMUS WITH CHICKEN TIKKA MASALA

scant 1 cup (7oz/200g) Greek yogurt

2 teaspoons ground coriander

2 teaspoons sweet mild paprika

1 teaspoon garam masala

1 teaspoon ground ginger

½ teaspoon ground cinnamon

¼ teaspoon chili powder

4 cardamom pods, crushed, black seeds ground in a mortar and pestle, green pods discarded

2 garlic cloves, finely chopped

2 tablespoons white wine vinegar or fresh lemon juice

1 tablespoon tomato paste

½ teaspoon sea salt

⅓ cup (2oz/55g) broken cashew nuts, plus a few extra to garnish

1½lb (650g) skinless, boneless chicken breasts, cubed

4 tablespoons (2oz/55g) unsalted butter

1 onion, minced (process in a food processor if you have one)

⅔ cup (5fl oz/150ml) heavy cream

2 cups (1lb/450g) Hummus (see p. 19), to serve

fresh cilantro leaves, torn, to garnish

FED UP WITH RICE? THEN TRY OUR TAKE ON THIS FAVORITE INDIAN CURRY. DON'T BE PUT OFF BY THE LONG LIST OF SPICES; CHANCES ARE YOU WILL HAVE MOST OF THEM ALREADY.

1 The day before serving or at least 7 hours in advance, put the yogurt into a large glass or ceramic shallow bowl. Add all the spices, garlic, vinegar or lemon juice, tomato paste, and salt and mix together with a spoon.

2 Preheat the oven to 300°F (150°C) or heat the broiler to medium.

3 Toast the cashew nut pieces, including a few extra ones for the garnish, either in the oven for 10 minutes, stirring from time to time until golden, or under the broiler for 4–5 minutes. Let cool, then process in a blender or food processor and stir into the yogurt marinade with the chicken, mixing well so that the chicken is evenly coated. Cover the dish with plastic wrap and chill in the refrigerator for 6 hours, or overnight.

4 The next day, heat the butter in a skillet, add the onion, and sauté gently for 3–4 minutes, stirring until just beginning to turn golden brown. Add the chicken and yogurt marinade to the pan and cook for 30–40 minutes, stirring from time to time, until the chicken is tender and cooked through. To check, lift one of the chicken pieces out of the pan, cut in half, and check there is no sign of pink juices.

5 Stir in the cream and warm through gently for 3 minutes. Spoon onto serving plates spread with Hummus and garnish with extra toasted cashew nuts and torn cilantro.

FALAFEL & WRAPS

SERVES 4–6
PREP: 20 MINUTES
CHILL: 30 MINUTES
COOK: 15 MINUTES

GREEN FALAFEL

1⅓ cups (9oz/250g) dried chickpeas, soaked overnight in cold water

1 white onion, coarsely chopped

small handful of fresh flat-leaf parsley

small handful of fresh mint sprigs, leaves torn from stems

small handful of fresh cilantro

2 garlic cloves, sliced

1 teaspoon ground cumin

1 teaspoon ground coriander

1 teaspoon baking soda

2 teaspoons black onion seeds

sea salt and freshly ground black pepper

3 tablespoons sesame seeds

4¼ cups (1¾ pints/1 liter) sunflower oil, for deep-frying

To serve:

Whole Wheat Pita Breads (see p. 110)

Hummus (see p. 19)

shredded lettuce

sliced tomatoes

Tahini Sauce (see p. 98) or Tzatziki (see p. 102) and Green Chili Sauce (see p. 104)

FALAFEL IS THE MIDDLE EASTERN VERSION OF FAST FOOD. THE BALLS CAN BE SERVED ON THEIR OWN, IN PITA OR A MEZZE, OR WITH A BOWL OF HUMMUS. WE OFTEN SERVE THEM ON A BED OF SHREDDED CABBAGE AND LETTUCE, WITH A TOMATO & CILANTRO SALSA (SEE P. 103), TZATZIKI (SEE P. 102), AND OLIVE OIL. A HAND GRINDER IS THE BEST PIECE OF EQUIPMENT FOR MAKING FALAFEL, BECAUSE PEOPLE TEND TO OVERPROCESS THE MIXTURE IN A FOOD PROCESSOR. FOR THE BEST TEXTURE, USE A GRINDER IF YOU HAVE ONE.

1 Drain the soaked chickpeas well in a colander.

2 If using a grinder, put all the ingredients, except the spices and seeds, through the grinder, and then mix together.

3 If using a food processor, process the onion, herbs, and garlic until finely chopped. Add the spices, baking soda, onion seeds, 1 teaspoon of salt, and black pepper to taste. Scoop into a bowl and set aside. Process the chickpeas gently until just broken up, in two batches if needed, then mix into the herb mixture.

4 Cover and chill in the refrigerator for 30 minutes.

5 Shape into 16–20 portions, then press firmly into balls with damp hands. Roll in the sesame seeds before frying.

6 Heat the oil for deep-frying in a saucepan to 350°F (180°C); a square of day-old bread should immediately sizzle in it. Lower four falafel into the oil and cook for 3–4 minutes until golden on the outside but so that you can still see the green of the herbs. Remove with a slotted spoon to a plate lined with paper towels. Test that they are done by cutting one in half; they should be cooked through and light and fluffy on the inside.

7 Check the temperature of the oil and continue frying the falafel, in batches, until they are all cooked. Serve tucked into Pita Breads, with Hummus, lettuce, tomatoes, and Tahini Sauce or Tzatziki and Green Chili Sauce.

NOTE

BEST MADE WITH DRIED SOAKED CHICKPEAS THAT ARE GROUND BEFORE COOKING FOR A LIGHTER TEXTURED FALAFEL. CANNED CHICKPEAS MAKE A WETTER MIXTURE WITH A DENSER TEXTURE.

SERVES 4–6
PREP: 30 MINUTES
CHILL: 30 MINUTES
COOK: 25–30 MINUTES

SWEET POTATO FALAFEL

1 large (9oz/250g) sweet potato, peeled and diced

1⅓ cups (9oz/250g) dried chickpeas, soaked overnight in cold water

1 onion, coarsely chopped

2 garlic cloves, sliced

1-inch (2.5-cm) piece fresh ginger, peeled and finely chopped

1 teaspoon ground turmeric

1 teaspoon ground coriander

1 teaspoon baking soda

sea salt and freshly ground black pepper

4¼ cups (1¾ pints/1 liter) sunflower oil, for deep-frying

To serve (optional):

2 cups (1lb/450g) Hummus (see p. 19)

1 quantity Tahini Sauce (see p. 98)

Mixed Vegetable Salad (see p. 88)

TRADITIONALISTS MAY THROW THEIR HANDS UP IN HORROR, BUT WE LIKE TO EXPERIMENT WITH DIFFERENT FLAVORED FALAFEL. WE HOPE YOU LIKE THIS DELICIOUS SWEET POTATO, GINGER, AND TURMERIC VERSION.

1 Pour water into the bottom of a steamer, bring to a boil, then add the sweet potato to the top of the steamer. Cover and cook for 10–15 minutes, depending on the size of the potato chunks, until tender when pierced with a knife.

2 Drain the chickpeas in a colander. Put the onion, garlic, and ginger into a food processor and finely chop. Add the ground spices, baking soda, 1 teaspoon of salt, and black pepper to taste and process together briefly. Scoop out into a bowl.

3 Put the chickpeas through a grinder, or add small batches of them to the food processor and briefly process until just broken up, scraping down the sides of the bowl every now and again. Transfer to the bowl, adding the sweet potato with the last batch of chickpeas.

4 Stir the falafel mix together, then cover and chill in the refrigerator for about 30 minutes.

5 Shape into 24 portions, then press firmly into balls with damp hands.

6 Heat the oil for deep-frying in a saucepan to 350°F (180°C); a square of day-old bread should immediately sizzle in it. Carefully lower four falafel into the oil and cook for 3–4 minutes until deep golden on the outside and light and fluffy on the inside. Remove with a slotted spoon to a plate lined with paper towels. Check the temperature of the oil and continue frying the falafel, in batches, until they are all cooked.

7 Serve on plates swirled with Hummus, drizzled with Tahini Sauce, and accompanied by some Mixed Vegetable Salad.

COOK'S TIP

IF YOU ARE MAKING LARGE BATCHES OF FALAFEL, YOU MIGHT WANT TO SHAPE THEM WITH A DAMP, SMALL ICE CREAM SCOOP AND FLATTEN THEM SLIGHTLY INTO PATTY SHAPES, BECAUSE THESE COOK MUCH QUICKER IN QUANTITY THAN BALLS.

SPICY RED FALAFEL

1¾ cups (9oz/250g) peeled and diced trimmed beets

1⅓ cups (9oz/250g) dried chickpeas, soaked overnight in plenty of cold water

1 red onion, coarsely chopped

2 garlic cloves, sliced

small handful of fresh cilantro, torn

1 large red chili, seeded and chopped

1 teaspoon paprika

1 teaspoon ground cumin

1 teaspoon baking soda

sea salt and freshly ground black pepper

4¼ cups (1¾ pints/1 liter) sunflower oil, for deep-frying

To serve (optional):

2 cups (1lb/450g) Hummus (see p. 19)

Tahini Sauce (see p. 98)

Tomato & Cilantro Salsa (see p. 103)

SERVES 4–6
PREP: 30 MINUTES
CHILL: 30 MINUTES
COOK: 35 MINUTES

BEETS ADD THE MOST AMAZING COLOR TO THESE HOT CHILI, CUMIN, AND PAPRIKA FALAFEL. FOR EXTRA HEAT, SERVE WITH TOMATO & CILANTRO SALSA (SEE P. 103) OR GREEN CHILI SAUCE (SEE P. 104), OR FOR THOSE WHO LOVE THAT HOT AND COLD SENSATION, TOP WITH SPOONFULS OF CREAMY TZATZIKI (SEE P. 102) AND SALT-PICKLED CUCUMBERS (SEE P. 146).

1 Pour water into the bottom of a steamer, bring to a boil, then add the beets to the top of the steamer. Cover and cook for 20 minutes, or until tender when pierced with a knife.

2 Drain the chickpeas in a colander. Put the onion, garlic, cilantro, and chili into a food processor and finely chop. Add the ground spices, baking soda, 1 teaspoon of salt, and black pepper to taste and process together briefly. Scoop out into a bowl.

3 Put the chickpeas through a grinder, or add small batches of them to the food processor and briefly process until just broken up, scraping down the sides of the bowl every now and again. Spoon into a bowl and set aside.

4 Process the beets until finely mashed. Stir into the chickpea mix, cover, and chill in the refrigerator for 30 minutes.

5 Shape into 24 portions, then press firmly into balls with damp hands.

6 Heat the oil for deep-frying in a saucepan to 350°F (180°C); a square of day-old bread should immediately sizzle in it. Carefully lower four falafel into the oil and cook for 3–4 minutes until deep golden on the outside and light and fluffy on the inside. Remove with a slotted spoon to a plate lined with paper towels. Check the temperature of the oil and continue frying the falafel, in batches, until they are all cooked.

7 Serve on plates swirled with Hummus, drizzled with Tahini Sauce and topped with Tomato & Cilantro Salsa.

MIXED BEAN FALAFEL

½ cup (3oz/85g) dried fava beans, soaked overnight in plenty of cold water

⅓ cup (3oz/85g) dried chickpeas, soaked overnight in plenty of cold water

½ cup (3oz/85g) dried green lentils, soaked overnight in plenty of cold water

1 onion, chopped

2 garlic cloves, sliced

small handful of fresh cilantro leaves, torn

grated zest and juice of 1 lemon

1 teaspoon ground allspice

1 teaspoon paprika

1 teaspoon baking soda

sea salt and freshly ground black pepper

4¼ cups (1¾ pints/1 liter) sunflower oil, for deep-frying

To serve (optional):

2 cups (1lb/450g) Hummus (see p. 19)

Tahini Sauce (see p. 98)

Fatoush (see p. 92)

SERVES 4–6
PREP: 30 MINUTES
CHILL: 30 MINUTES
COOK: 15 MINUTES

FALAFEL DON'T HAVE TO BE MADE JUST WITH CHICKPEAS. A MIXTURE OF CHICKPEAS, FAVA BEANS, AND LENTILS ALSO TASTE GREAT WHEN FLAVORED WITH TANGY LEMON AND A LITTLE GROUND ALLSPICE.

1 Drain the fava beans, chickpeas, and lentils well in a colander. Put the onion, garlic, and cilantro leaves into a food processor and process until finely chopped. Add the lemon zest, ground spices, baking soda, 1 teaspoon of salt, and black pepper to taste and process together briefly. Scoop into a bowl and set aside.

2 Put the drained (soaked) legumes through a grinder, or add small batches of them to the food processor and briefly process until just broken up, scraping down the sides of the bowl every now and again. Gradually mix in more of the legumes and the lemon juice until they are a coarse paste.

3 Mix the legume mixture into the onion mixture. Cover and chill in the refrigerator for 30 minutes.

4 Shape into 24 portions, then press firmly into balls with damp hands.

5 Heat the oil for deep-frying in a saucepan to 350°F (180°C); a square of day-old bread should immediately sizzle in it. Carefully lower four falafel into the oil and cook for 3–4 minutes until deep golden on the outside and light and fluffy on the inside. Remove with a slotted spoon to a plate lined with paper towels. Check the temperature of the oil and continue frying the falafel, in batches, until they are all cooked.

6 Serve on plates swirled with Hummus, drizzled with the Green Tahini Sauce and accompanied by the Fatoush salad.

FALAFEL WRAPS

4¼ cups (1¾ pints/1 liter) sunflower oil, for deep-frying

8 shaped but not cooked Falafel (see p. 56)

2 large flat wraps

½ cup (½oz/100g) Hummus (see p. 19)

Salt-Pickled Cucumbers (see p. 146) or store-bought pickles

Tahini Sauce (see p. 98)

1 large tomato, thinly sliced

cabbage or lettuce, thinly sliced

Green Chili Sauce (see p. 104)

═══
SERVES 2
PREP: 15 MINUTES
COOK: 6–8 MINUTES
═══

FALAFEL IS ONE OF THOSE DISHES THAT DOESN'T TASTE AMAZING ON ITS OWN; IT NEEDS TO BE BALANCED WITH OTHER INGREDIENTS. THAT'S WHY WRAPS OR PITA POCKETS WORK SO WELL. THE ESSENTIAL COMPONENTS OF A FALAFEL WRAP ARE: HUMMUS (TEXTURE), TOMATO (ACIDITY), CHILI SAUCE (SPICE), TAHINI SAUCE (LEMONY), AND PICKLED CUCUMBERS (SALTY) WITH SOME CABBAGE OR LETTUCE (FOR CRUNCH). OPTIONAL INGREDIENTS INCLUDE GUACAMOLE, FRIED EGGPLANT SLICES, PICKLED BEETS OR OTHER ROOT VEG, AND FRIES.

RONEN: MY FAVORITE FALAFEL CAME FROM A LITTLE SHOP IN TEL AVIV CALLED "THE QUEENS OF FALAFEL." OWNED BY TWO LADIES, THEY SERVED THREE TYPES: GREEN (CILANTRO AND PARSLEY), ORANGE (SWEET POTATO), AND RED (CHILIS). SEE THE CONNECTION? THE PITA BREAD WAS ALWAYS SO MOIST AND CHEWY AND THE FALAFEL BALLS MELTED INTO THE BREAD WONDERFULLY. UNFORTUNATELY, THEY CLOSED DOWN A FEW YEARS AGO, BUT LUCKILY WE'D OPENED OUR FIRST BRANCH BY THEN, SO I COULD EAT OURS EVERY DAY.

1 Heat the oil for deep-frying in a saucepan to 350°F (180°C); a square of day-old bread should immediately sizzle in it. Cook the Falafel, in batches, for 3–4 minutes until browned and crisp on the outside and light and fluffy on the inside. Remove with a slotted spoon to a plate lined with paper towels.

2 Warm the wraps, one at a time, in a hot dry skillet for 1–2 minutes each. Transfer to a large board, spread with the Hummus, top with the hot Falafel, Pickled Cucumbers, tomato slices, and cabbage or lettuce. Drizzle with Tahini Sauce and Green Chili Sauce. Fold each wrap around the Falafel to make a package, then serve.

SABICH: EGGPLANT & EGG WRAP

2 hard-boiled eggs, cooked for 8 hours

1 eggplant, cut into long thin slices

sea salt

¼ cup (2fl oz/60ml) sunflower oil

2 large flat wraps

½ cup (3½oz/100g) Hummus (see p. 19)

¼ quantity Tomato & Cilantro Salsa (see p. 103)

few slices of Salt-Pickled Cucumber (see p. 146) or store-bought pickle, sliced lengthwise

1 quantity Tahini Sauce (see p. 98)

To serve:
Tzatziki (see p. 102)

SERVES 2
PREP: 45 MINUTES
(PLUS 8 HOURS FOR
THE EGGS,
IF DESIRED)
COOK: 6-8 MINUTES

THIS IRAQI SPECIALITY IS MADE WITH EGGS THAT HAVE BEEN COOKED LONG AND SLOW. YOU CAN BOIL THEM FOR JUST 2–3 HOURS, IF YOU PREFER, BUT IN THE RESTAURANT WE COOK THEM FOR 8 HOURS. DON'T BE ALARMED WHEN YOU PEEL AND CUT INTO THEM. THE EGG WHITES WILL BE A BROWNISH COLOR, BUT THEY WILL ALSO BE RICH IN CALCIUM, WHICH WILL HAVE BEEN ABSORBED FROM THE SHELL. JUST REMEMBER TO WATCH THE PAN AND TOP UP WITH WARM WATER WHEN THE LEVEL GETS A LITTLE LOW—IT'S EASY TO FORGET ABOUT THEM AND BOIL THE PAN DRY. IF STRETCHED FOR TIME, GET THE COLOR MORE QUICKLY BY THROWING A TEA BAG INTO THE WATER.

1 Peel the eggs, cut each into four wedges, and set aside.

2 Spread the eggplant slices out on some paper towels, sprinkle with salt, and let "sweat" for 30 minutes. Then rinse and pat dry.

3 Heat the oil in a large skillet and sauté the eggplant slices on both sides for 4–5 minutes until golden. Alternatively, brush the slices with a little oil and cook under a preheated broiler.

4 Warm the wraps in the dried eggplant pan, then take out and put on plates. Spread each one with some of the Hummus, then top with the eggplant slices. Spoon the Tomato & Cilantro Salsa on top, then add the egg and Pickled Cucumbers. Finally, drizzle with plenty of Tahini Sauce.

5 Fold the wraps tightly around the fillings, turn over so that the seams are underneath on the plate, cut in half, and serve with Tzatziki on the side.

BEEF WRAPS

4 large flat wraps
1 cup (8oz/225g) Hummus (see p. 19)
4 romaine lettuce leaves
¼ quantity Tomato & Cilantro Salsa
(see p. 103)
2 Salt-Pickled Cucumbers (see p. 146)
or store-bought pickles, drained
and cut into long strips
1 quantity hot beef casserole from
Hummus with Chunky Beef
(see p. 35)

SERVES 4
PREP: 15 MINUTES
COOK:
3 MINUTES

TRANSFORM SOME LEFTOVER BEEF CASSEROLE INTO
LUNCH OR ANOTHER DINNER WITH THESE TASTY WRAPS.
OR WHY NOT MAKE A DOUBLE QUANTITY OF CASSEROLE AND
FREEZE IN SMALLER PORTIONS FOR ANOTHER NIGHT WHEN
YOU ARE TOO TIRED TO COOK FROM SCRATCH.

1 Warm the wraps in a hot dry skillet for 1 minute on each side, then remove and put on serving plates.

2 Spread the Hummus in a line down the center of each wrap, top with 1 romaine lettuce leaf, broken in half, then add a spoonful of Tomato & Cilantro Salsa, two long strips of Salt-Pickled Cucumber, then, finally, top with a couple of spoonfuls of the hot beef.

3 Fold the ends of the wrap inward, then use a sheet of nonstick parchment paper to roll the wrap up tightly. The paper helps keep the wrap together. Tuck the ends of the paper in like a package, then cut the wrap in half, with the paper still in place, to serve.

SOUPS

SERVES 4
PREP: 10 MINUTES
COOK: 50 MINUTES

CHICKPEA & CHORIZO SOUP

2 tablespoons olive oil

2 onions, finely chopped

4 garlic cloves, finely chopped

5½-oz (150-g) piece chorizo sausage, sliced

3 baking potatoes, peeled and diced

1 (15-oz/425-g) can chickpeas, rinsed and drained

½ teaspoon hot paprika or chili powder

4¼ cups (1¾ pints/1 liter) chicken or vegetable stock or broth

sea salt and freshly ground black pepper

warm bread, to serve

SPANISH CHORIZO IS ONE OF THOSE INGREDIENTS THAT CAN TURN EVERYDAY, MUNDANE INGREDIENTS INTO SOMETHING SPECIAL. IT KEEPS IN THE REFRIGERATOR FOR SEVERAL WEEKS AND MAKES A GREAT BASE FOR THIS HEARTY SOUP-CUM-STEW.

1 Heat the oil in a medium saucepan, add the onions, and sauté over medium heat for 10 minutes, stirring from time to time, until just beginning to soften. Add the garlic, chorizo, and potatoes and sauté for another 10 minutes until the onion and potatoes have been browned with the juices from the chorizo.

2 Stir in the chickpeas and paprika or chili powder, stock, and a generous sprinkling of salt and black pepper. Bring to a boil, then cover with a lid, lower the heat, and simmer for 30 minutes, stirring from time to time.

3 Ladle into bowls and serve with warm bread.

SERVES 4
PREP: 15 MINUTES
COOK: 42 MINUTES

TOMATO SOUP
WITH PITA BREAD CROUTONS

1 tablespoon olive oil

1 red onion, chopped

1 Yukon gold or white round potato, peeled and diced

10 tomatoes (about 1½lb/650g), peeled and coarsely chopped

4 garlic cloves, finely chopped

1 tablespoon dried oregano

1 tablespoon fresh thyme, chopped

3¼ cups (1¼ pints/750ml) vegetable stock or broth

1 tablespoon tomato paste

2 teaspoons granulated sugar

sea salt and freshly ground black pepper

fresh basil leaves, to garnish

For the pita bread croutons:

2 Pita Breads (see p. 110), cut into ¾-inch (2-cm) squares

2 tablespoons olive oil

2 garlic cloves, finely chopped

1 teaspoon dried oregano

EVERY COUNTRY HAS A FAVORITE VERSION OF TOMATO SOUP. WE LIKE OURS FLAVORED WITH GARLIC, OREGANO, AND THYME AND LEFT CHUNKY, BUT FOR THOSE SMOOTH OPERATORS OUT THERE, FEEL FREE TO PROCESS YOURS IN A FOOD PROCESSOR OR BLENDER BEFORE SERVING.

1 To make the soup, heat the oil in a large saucepan, add the onion and potato and cook over medium heat for 10 minutes, stirring from time to time, until just beginning to soften and to turn pale golden.

2 Mix in the tomatoes, garlic, oregano, and thyme and cook for 2–3 minutes, then add the stock, tomato paste, sugar, and a generous sprinkling of salt and black pepper. Bring to a boil, then cover with a lid, lower the heat, and simmer for 30 minutes, stirring from time to time, until the tomatoes are pulpy.

3 For the croutons, preheat the oven to 400°F (200°C).

4 Put the Pita Breads into a small roasting pan, drizzle with the oil, then sprinkle with the garlic and oregano. Gently turn the bread until evenly coated in the oil, then spread out into an even layer and bake for 8–10 minutes until crisp.

5 Roughly mash or puree the soup in a blender to taste, then reheat, if needed. Ladle the soup into bowls, sprinkle with fresh basil, and top with the warm croutons.

COOK'S TIP

To make this soup creamy, add ½ cup (3½fl oz/100ml) light cream toward the end of cooking.

SPICY LENTIL SOUP

1¼ cups (9oz/250g) dried red or green lentils

2 tablespoons olive oil

1 large fresh or dried bay leaf

3 garlic cloves, finely chopped

½–1 large red chili, seeded and finely chopped

1 large red onion, finely chopped

1 teaspoon ground cumin

5 cups (2 pints/1.2 liters) chicken or vegetable stock or broth

sea salt and freshly ground black pepper

small handful of fresh cilantro, chopped

warm bread, to serve

sour cream, to garnish

SERVES 4
PREP: 15 MINUTES
COOK: 16–26 MINUTES

MADE WITH JUST A FEW HUMBLE INGREDIENTS, THIS SOUP WILL ONLY BE AS GOOD AS THE STOCK OR BROTH THAT YOU USE. PREFERABLY USE HOMEMADE STOCK OR BROTH, BUT A GOOD LOW-SALT CUBE IS FINE. IF YOU HAVE THE REMAINS OF A ROASTED CHICKEN, SIMMER IT IN WATER WITH SOME ONIONS, CARROTS, AND HERBS FOR AN HOUR OR SO, THEN STRAIN AND USE AS THE BASE FOR THIS COMFORTING SOUP.

1 Rinse the lentils well in cold water, then let drain in a strainer. Heat the oil in a medium saucepan, add the bay leaf, garlic, and half the chili, and sauté over low heat for 1 minute to release the flavors. Stir in the onion and sauté for 5 minutes, stirring from time to time, until softened.

2 Mix in the drained lentils and cook for 2 minutes. Add the cumin and season well with salt and black pepper. Add the stock, then bring to a boil, cover with a lid, lower the heat, and simmer for 10–15 minutes, adding extra stock or water, if needed, until the lentils are tender.

3 Stir in the chopped cilantro, then taste and adjust the seasoning, mixing in the remaining chili or adding extra salt and black pepper. Ladle into bowls and serve with warm bread. Garnish with a dollop of sour cream in each bowl.

MIXED BEAN & BACON SOUP

1 tablespoon olive oil

1 red onion, chopped

4oz (115g) bacon slices, cut into strips

4 frankfurters, sliced

2 smoked Kabanos Polish sausages, sliced

4 garlic cloves, crushed

2 carrots, thinly sliced

4¼ cups (1¾ pints/1 liter) chicken or vegetable stock or broth

1 (15-oz/425-g) can kidney beans, rinsed and drained

1 (15-oz/425-g) can lima beans, rinsed and drained

1 (15-oz/425-g) can chickpeas, rinsed and drained

1 (16-oz/450-g) can baked beans

3 tablespoons sweet mild paprika

sea salt and freshly ground black pepper

2 tablespoons sunflower oil

2 tablespoons all-purpose flour

½ each red and green bell pepper, cored, seeded, and diced

warm bread, to serve

SERVES 8
PREP: 15 MINUTES
COOK: 25 MINUTES

RONEN: THIS IS ONE OF MY MOM'S MOST PRIZED RECIPES, TRIED AND TESTED IN THE RESTAURANTS. IF YOU HAVEN'T HAD TIME TO SHOP OR YOU'RE A LITTLE LOW ON FUNDS, TRY THIS MAIN-DISH SOUP MADE WITH CANNED BEANS, FRESH VEGETABLES, AND CHOPPED BACON, PEPPED UP WITH SWEET PAPRIKA. IF YOU LIKE A LITTLE CHILI HEAT, CHOOSE SMOKED HOT PAPRIKA, WHICH IS AVAILABLE IN LARGER SUPERMARKETS.

1 Heat the oil in a medium saucepan, add the onion, and sauté for 5 minutes, stirring from time to time, until just beginning to soften. Mix in the bacon, frankfurters, Kabanos, garlic, and carrots and cook for 5 minutes, or until the bacon is just beginning to turn golden and the carrots soften.

2 Stir in the stock and all the beans and stock, season with paprika, salt, and black pepper, and bring to a boil, stirring. Cover with a lid, lower the heat, and simmer for 10 minutes.

3 Meanwhile, in a separate small saucepan, heat the sunflower oil, add the flour, and stir until golden. Add to the simmering soup, stir for 2 minutes until thickened and smooth, then turn off the heat.

4 Finally, stir in the chopped bell peppers (they don't need to cook down, they should be crunchy), then ladle the soup into serving bowls and serve with warm bread.

JERUSALEM ARTICHOKE SOUP
WITH CHESTNUT CREAM

2 tablespoons sunflower oil

1 large white onion, chopped

12oz (350g) Jerusalem artichokes

sea salt and freshly ground black pepper

4 garlic cloves, chopped

2½ cups (1 pint/600ml) good vegetable stock or broth

1 (7-oz/200-g) package prepared chestnuts

⅔ cup (5fl oz/150ml) whipping cream

handful of fresh chives, snipped (optional)

SERVES 4
PREP: 20 MINUTES
COOK: 40 MINUTES

JERUSALEM ARTICHOKES DON'T LOOK PROMISING, BUT THEY MAKE THE MOST WONDERFUL VELVETY SMOOTH SOUP WITH A LIGHT, DELICATE FLAVOR ALL OF THEIR OWN. PROCESSING PREPARED CHESTNUTS WITH CREAM ADDS A KIND OF GLAM TOPPING THAT TASTES FABULOUS SPOONED INTO THE CENTER OF THE SOUP BEFORE BEING TOPPED WITH SOME EXTRA CRUMBLED CHESTNUTS OR SNIPPED FRESH CHIVES.

1 Heat the oil in a medium saucepan, add the onion, and sauté for 5 minutes over low heat, stirring from time to time, until softened but not browned.

2 Meanwhile, peel and slice the Jerusalem artichokes. They discolor quickly so do this at the last minute, then rinse with cold water, drain, and slice. Add the artichokes to the onion with a pinch of salt and sauté over low heat for 5 minutes, stirring from time to time, until just beginning to soften.

3 Stir in the garlic, then pour in the stock and bring to a boil, stirring. Cover with a lid, lower the heat, and simmer for 20–30 minutes until the artichokes are tender.

4 Meanwhile, crush half the chestnuts with an immersion blender or fork and gradually stir into the cream until smooth. Spoon into a bowl and chill until needed.

5 Process the soup still in the pan with an immersion blender or transfer to a blender and blend. Taste and adjust the seasoning, if needed, then reheat and ladle into small bowls. Add a spoonful of the chestnut cream to the center of each and top with a few remaining chestnuts, crumbled into small pieces. Some snipped fresh chives also work well as a garnish.

ROASTED EGGPLANT SALAD

3 large eggplants
1 lemon, halved
sea salt
Tahini Sauce (see p. 98)
chopped fresh parsley, for sprinkling
olive oil, for drizzling

For the Dip (optional):

3 large eggplants
1 red bell pepper, halved, seeded, and finely diced
3 fresh thyme sprigs, leaves only, chopped (about 1 tablespoon)
3 tablespoons chopped fresh oregano or ¼ teaspoon dried
sea salt and freshly ground black pepper
2 tablespoons olive oil
juice of ½ lemon
2 tablespoons Tahini Sauce (see p. 98)

To garnish:

½ pomegranate, seeds removed from casing (optional)
3 tablespoons chopped fresh flat-leaf parsley

To serve:

warm Pita Breads (see p. 110)
bell pepper, carrot, and cucumber sticks

SERVES 4
PREP: 15 MINUTES
COOK:
30–40 MINUTES

YOU CAN EAT THIS WITH TAHINI (LEBANESE-STYLE), WITH YOGURT (TURKISH-STYLE), OR SIMPLY WITH LOADS OF LEMON AND A LITTLE GARLIC. OUR FAVORITE IS WITH TAHINI—IT'S A MATCH MADE IN HEAVEN. IN THE MIDDLE EAST, THE CHARRED EGGPLANTS ARE SIMPLY THROWN DOWN INTO THE MIDDLE OF THE TABLE AND EVERYONE DIGS IN WITH THEIR SPOONS, FIGHTING FOR THE LAST PIECES OF SUCCULENT FLESH. WE HAVE ALSO ADDED A VARIATION TO TURN THE COOKED EGGPLANT INTO A BABA GANOUSH–STYLE DIP TO SERVE AS PART OF A MEZZE SPREAD.

1 Char the eggplants directly over a stove-top gas flame. No need for a rack; just put them straight on top with the heat on medium. Cook for 15–20 minutes, turning with tongs as the skin blackens, cracks, and white ash spots begin to appear, until the skin is the same all over. They will puff up as they cook and some steam may escape, so pay attention and don't overburn them. If you don't have a gas stove, preheat the broiler to high. Remove the broiler rack and cook the eggplants directly in the pan, checking that they are about 1 inch (2.5cm) away from the heat source. Broil for 30–45 minutes, turning them several times until the skin is blackened and papery and beginning to turn ash white.

2 Transfer the hot eggplants to a cutting board or large plate, make a slit along the lengths, and open out. Squeeze in the lemon juice, flavor with a little salt, LOTS of Tahini Sauce, and a little parsley, then drizzle with olive oil. Give guests teaspoons to scoop the delicious warm flesh from the skins. Don't worry if you eat the skin—it all adds to the amazing flavor. One lucky guest can bite into the head of the eggplant to extract the best part.

3 To make the Baba Ganoush Dip, cook the eggplants as above, then let cool. When completely cold, slit in half, scoop the flesh out, then coarsely chop. Add to a bowl, stir in the diced red bell pepper, thyme, oregano, and salt and black pepper to taste. Drizzle with the oil, lemon juice, and Tahini Sauce to taste, then toss gently together. Garnish with pomegranate seeds and parsley. Serve with Pita Breads and vegetable sticks.

SERVES 4
PREP: 15 MINUTES
COOK: 1 HOUR

ROASTED VEGETABLE SALAD

2 large red onions (about 9oz/250g), cut into large chunks

2 sweet potatoes (about 1½lb/650g), peeled and cut into 1-inch (2.5-cm) chunks

3 tablespoons packed light brown sugar

2 garlic cloves, coarsely chopped

¼ cup (2fl oz/60ml) olive oil

sea salt and freshly ground black pepper

½ green cabbage (about 12oz/350g), cut into large chunks

2 large zucchini (about 14oz/400g), cut into large chunks

⅓ cup (1oz/25g) coarsely chopped fresh flat-leaf parsley

½ cup (4fl oz/120ml) Yellow Sauce (see p. 106)

THIS SLOW ROASTED MIX OF RED ONION, SWEET POTATO, AND ZUCCHINI HAS A SURPRISE ADDITION OF GREEN CABBAGE— NOT NORMALLY AN INGREDIENT YOU THINK OF TO ROAST, BUT IT WORKS WELL IN A WINTERY SALAD SPRINKLED WITH PLENTY OF CHOPPED PARSLEY AND SERVED WITH OUR SERIOUSLY GARLICKY YELLOW SAUCE (SEE P. 106).

1 Preheat the oven to 300°F (150°C).

2 Put the red onions and sweet potatoes into a roasting pan. Sprinkle with the sugar and half the garlic, then drizzle with 2 tablespoons of the oil and season with salt and black pepper. Using your hands, toss the vegetables in the oil and sugar mix until they are evenly coated.

3 Put the green cabbage and zucchini into a separate roasting pan, sprinkle with the remaining garlic and the olive oil, then add salt and black pepper and mix together.

4 Roast all the vegetables for about 1 hour, turning once or twice, until they are soft and lightly browned. Remove from the oven and let cool.

5 Transfer the roasted vegetables to a serving bowl, sprinkle with the chopped parsley, and spoon the Yellow Sauce over the top.

TABOULEH

PACKED WITH CHOPPED MINT AND PARSLEY (YOU'RE AIMING FOR HALF HERBS TO BULGUR), THIS LEMON-DRESSED BULGUR OR CRACKED WHEAT SALAD IS GREAT SERVED WITH VIRTUALLY ANY SAVORY MAIN DISH, OR AS A SIMPLE APPETIZER WITH BABY ROMAINE LETTUCE LEAVES TO SCOOP IT UP.

¾ cup (3½oz/100g) fine bulgur wheat
¼ cup (2fl oz/60ml) virgin olive oil
juice of 1 lemon
sea salt and freshly ground black pepper
½ cup (1oz/25g) finely chopped fresh mint
1 cup (2oz/55g) fresh flat-leaf parsley
2 plum tomatoes, finely diced
¼ cucumber, diced
½ bunch of scallions, finely chopped
½ pomegranate, seeds removed from casing

1 Put the bulgur wheat into a bowl, cover with cold salted water, and let soak for at least 30 minutes until softened.

2 Drain the bulgur wheat, if required, and spoon into a salad bowl.

3 Add the chopped herbs, tomatoes, cucumber, and scallions to the bulgur wheat, stirring gently.

4 Using a fork, stir the oil, lemon juice, and a generous sprinkling of salt and pepper together in a small bowl. Only add the dressing just as you are about to serve., sprinkling the pomegranate seeds on top.

SERVES 4
PREP: 15 MINUTES
SOAK: 30 MINUTES
COOK: 10 MINUTES

MIXED VEGETABLE SALAD

1 red bell pepper, halved, cored, seeded, and cut into ¾-inch (2-cm) dice

½ cucumber, skin partly peeled, halved, and seeded, if desired, then cut into ¾-inch (2-cm) dice

10–12 cherry tomatoes on the vine (about 8oz/225g), halved

For the dressing:
¼ cup (½oz/15g) finely chopped fresh flat-leaf parsley

1 garlic clove, finely chopped
2 tablespoons white wine vinegar
2 tablespoons olive oil
1 tablespoon honey
1 teaspoon granulated sugar
sea salt and coarsely ground black pepper

YOU CAN TRANSFORM THESE EVERYDAY VEGETABLES INTO A COLORFUL SIDE DISH WITH THIS TANGY DRESSING. WHEN WE MAKE UP LARGE QUANTITIES OF THE DRESSING FOR THE RESTAURANT, WE PROCESS THE INGREDIENTS IN A BLENDER. HOWEVER, THIS DOMESTIC QUANTITY MAY BE TOO SMALL FOR YOUR PROCESSOR, BUT IF YOU HAVE A MINI BOWL OR SPICE MILL ATTACHMENT, THEN THIS WOULD WORK FINE. UNLIKE LETTUCE-BASE SALADS, THIS ONE TASTES JUST AS GOOD THE NEXT DAY, SO IT'S GREAT TO PACK INTO A SMALL CONTAINER FOR LUNCH BAGS, KEEPING THE DRESSING ON THE SIDE.

1 Put the red bell pepper, cucumber, and tomatoes into a salad bowl and toss together.

2 For the dressing, add the parsley to a bowl with the garlic, vinegar, and oil. Mix in the honey and sugar, then generously season with salt and black pepper. Alternatively, process in a blender or spice mill.

3 Spoon the dressing over the salad and toss together gently before serving.

SERVES 4
PREP: 15 MINUTES

FALAFEL SALAD

oil, for deep-frying

1 quantity shaped but uncooked Falafel (see p. 19)

4 cups (14oz/400g) finely shredded green cabbage

½ romaine lettuce, leaves separated and shredded

salt

1 quantity Tomato & Cilantro Salsa (see p. 103)

1 quantity Tzatziki (see p. 102)

2 tablespoons olive oil, for drizzling

FALAFELS ARE VERY ADDICTIVE, BUT THEY'RE FRIED, SO NEED TO BE BALANCED IN A SALAD. HERE, WE BALANCE THEIR TEXTURE AND TASTE BY ADDING CABBAGE FOR CRUNCH, TOMATOES FOR ACIDITY, CILANTRO FOR FRESHNESS, AND TZATZIKI TO OFFSET THE OIL. YOU WON'T FIND THIS COMBINATION ELSEWHERE (BECAUSE IT'S NOT A TRADITIONAL WAY TO EAT FALAFEL) BUT WE THINK IT WORKS.

1 Heat the oil for deep-frying in a saucepan to 350°F (180°C); a square of day-old bread should immediately sizzle in it. Lower three Falafel into the oil and cook for 3–4 minutes until golden on the outside but so that you can still see the green of the herbs. Remove with a slotted spoon to a plate lined with paper towels. Test that they are done by cutting one in half; they should be cooked through and light and fluffy on the inside. Continue frying the Falafel, in batches, checking the temperature of the oil from time to time.

2 Divide the shredded cabbage and lettuce among the plates, season with salt, then top with spoonfuls of the salsa and Tzatziki. Drizzle with a little olive oil, then arrange the Falafel on the Tzatziki and serve.

SERVES 4
PREP: 15 MINUTES
COOK: 10 MINUTES

GREEK SALAD

1 red or green bell pepper, halved, seeded, and diced

½ cucumber, partly peeled, seeded if desired, and diced

8–10 cherry tomatoes on the vine (about 7oz/200g), halved

1 red onion, thinly sliced

⅓ cup (3½oz/100g) drained feta cheese

¼ teaspoon dried oregano

3 tablespoons olive oil

A CLASSIC AND ALL-TIME FAVORITE, THIS SALAD IS FRESH TASTING, CRISP, CRUNCHY, AND PRETTY CHUNKY, TOO. GREEKS PUT A SLAB OF FETA ON TOP OF THE SALAD, BUT WE FIND THAT CRUMBLING THE FETA HELPS IT REACH ALL PARTS OF THE SALAD AND MAKES IT BETTER FOR SHARING. FETA IS SALTY, SO THERE'S NO NEED TO ADD EXTRA SALT—JUST SEASON WITH PLENTY OF DRIED OREGANO.

FOR AN ADDED DIMENSION, TRY ADDING SOME CAPERS AND CAPER LEAVES.

1 Put the green bell pepper, cucumber, tomatoes, and onion into a salad bowl and toss together gently. Crumble the feta into small pieces with your fingertips or dice if you prefer. Sprinkle the cheese over the salad with the dried oregano, then drizzle with the oil and serve.

SERVES 4
PREP: 15 MINUTES

FATOUSH

THIS CRISP CRUNCHY SALAD IS A GREAT WAY TO USE UP THOSE LAST ONE OR TWO LEFTOVER PITA BREADS. BAKE THEM IN THE OVEN UNTIL CRISP AND THEN FINISH WITH A DRIZZLE OF OLIVE OIL AND ZA'ATAR SPICES—A POPULAR SPICE MIX MADE WITH THYME, OREGANO, AND OUR FAVORITE SESAME SEEDS.

For the pita bread croutons:

2 Whole Wheat Pita Breads (see p. 110) or store bought

2–3 tablespoons olive oil

up to 2 teaspoons Za'atar Spice Blend if made with dried herbs or 2 tablespoons if made with fresh herbs (see below)

For the salad:

1 small iceberg lettuce, cut into bite-size pieces

1 green bell pepper, halved, cored, seeded, and diced

½ bunch of scallions, thinly sliced

¼ cucumber, diced

2 tomatoes, diced

handful of fresh parsley, finely chopped

handful of fresh mint, finely chopped

For the dressing:

¼ cup (2fl oz/60ml) olive oil

juice of 1 lemon

1 teaspoon sumac seeds, finely crushed

sea salt and freshly ground black pepper

SERVES 4
PREP: 15 MINUTES
COOK: 30–35 MINUTES

1 Preheat the oven to 300°F (150°C).

2 Cut the Pita Breads into ¾-inch (2-cm) squares, sprinkle them over a baking sheet, then drizzle with the oil and sprinkle with the za'atar. Bake for 25–30 minutes, checking every 10 minutes or so, turning the squares and moving them around so that they dry evenly.

3 Meanwhile, put all the salad ingredients into a large salad bowl and toss together gently.

4 Put all the dressing ingredients into a small bowl and stir together with a fork. Alternatively, put everything into a screw-top jar, screw on the lid, and shake to mix.

5 Pour the dressing over the salad and toss gently together. Sprinkle over the hot croutons and serve immediately.

ZA'ATAR SPICE BLEND

Toast 1 tablespoon of sesame seeds in a dry skillet until just beginning to brown, then pound with a pestle in a mortar. Mix in 1 teaspoon each of dried thyme and oregano and ½ teaspoon of salt. This mix will keep in a screw-top jar in the refrigerator for up to a month.

SERVES 4
PREP: 15 MINUTES
COOK: 10 MINUTES

CAULIFLOWER WITH GREEN TAHINI

1 large cauliflower (or 2 small ones)

⅔ cup (1½oz/40g) finely chopped fresh flat-leaf parsley

2 large garlic cloves, finely chopped

1 quantity Tahini Sauce (see p. 98)

4¼ cups (1¾ pints/1 liter) canola oil, for deep-frying

1 lemon, cut into wedges

sea salt

THE BRITISH GROW LOADS OF CAULIFLOWERS, BUT IT IS ONE OF THOSE INGREDIENTS THAT IS RARELY SERVED AND WHEN IT'S COOKED, TENDS JUST TO BE PLAIN BOILED OR SMOTHERED IN A CHEESE SAUCE. THIS SALAD OF CRISPY DEEP-FRIED CAULIFLOWER FLORETS, SERVED ON A BED OF PARSLEY-SPECKLED GARLIC TAHINI SAUCE, LIFTS THIS HUMBLE VEGETABLE TO A WHOLE NEW LEVEL.

1 Cut any leaves from the cauliflower, cut in half, and then cut away the florets and discard the woody core. Cut any larger florets into even bite-size florets so they will all cook in the same time.

2 Stir the parsley and garlic into the Tahini Sauce and set aside.

3 Pour the oil for deep-frying into a medium saucepan so that the pan is filled only halfway, then heat the oil to 325°F (160°C). Alternatively, test by adding a cauliflower floret to the hot oil; when it is hot enough, the oil should immediately sizzle around the cauliflower.

4 Add the cauliflower to the hot oil, a few pieces at a time, until about one-third of the florets are in the oil. Don't overcrowd the pan or the oil temperature will drop too much. Deep-fry for 2–3 minutes until the cauliflower is browned, then scoop out of the pan with a slotted spoon and transfer to a plate lined with paper towels. Bring the oil back to temperature, then continue cooking the cauliflower, in small batches, until all the florets are done. Let cool for a few minutes.

5 Spoon the Tahini Sauce over four serving plates, then top with the cauliflower. Squeeze a little lemon juice over the top, season with salt to taste, and serve immediately. Or serve in separate bowls for your guests to mix themselves.

BREADS & SAUCES

TAHINI SAUCE

¾ cup (6oz/175g) tahini

2 tablespoons freshly squeezed
lemon juice, plus extra to serve

sea salt, to taste

½ cup (4fl oz/125ml) cold water

To serve:

1 quantity Green Chili Sauce
(see p. 104)

4 Whole Wheat Pita Breads
(see p. 110),
warmed and cut into strips

TAHINI IS THE BASIS OF ALL LEVANTINE CUISINE AND IS AVAILABLE IN JARS FROM HEALTH FOOD STORES AND LARGER SUPERMARKETS. MAKE SURE YOU MASTER THE BASIC ART OF HANDLING THIS INGREDIENT; IT BEHAVES LIKE QUICKSAND AT FIRST, SO READ THE INSTRUCTIONS CAREFULLY. OUR FAVORITE WAY TO SERVE THIS DELICIOUS SAUCE IS AS AN APPETIZER SPREAD OVER SMALL PLATES, DRIZZLED WITH GREEN CHILI SAUCE (SEE P. 104) AND A SQUEEZE OF FRESH LEMON JUICE WITH WARM PITA BREADS (SEE P. 110) TO SCOOP IT UP.

1 Put the tahini, lemon juice, and salt to taste into a bowl and gradually mix in the cold water with a wooden spoon. The mixture will behave a little like quicksand and become firmer the more water you add. While it is still hard, taste it to see whether it needs more lemon or salt and add, if necessary.

2 Continue slowly adding the water. When almost all the water is added, the tahini will start to soften as it becomes saturated but will still be a thick, spreadable paste like softly whipped cream.

3 Spoon onto small serving plates, spread into an even layer with the back of a spoon, then drizzle with Green Chili Sauce and serve with warm Pita Bread strips.

VARIATION

For green tahini sauce, stir 2 finely chopped garlic cloves and ⅓ cup (¾oz/20g) chopped fresh parsley into the main recipe.

SERVES 4
MAKES 1⅓ CUPS (10½OZ/300G)
PREP: 10 MINUTES

SERVES 4–6
PREP: 10 MINUTES

GUACAMOLE

2 avocados, halved, pitted, peeled, and cut into ½-inch/1-cm dice

2 plum tomatoes, halved and finely chopped

½ red bell pepper, cored, seeded, and finely chopped

½ red onion, finely chopped

2 scallions, finely chopped

small bunch of fresh flat-leaf parsley, or cilantro finely chopped

2 tablespoons olive oil

juice of 1 lemon

sea salt and freshly ground black pepper

To serve (optional):

2 cups (1lb/450g) Hummus (see p. 19)

paprika, for sprinkling

fresh parsley, chopped, to garnish

AVOCADOS TURN BROWN EVEN WHEN TOSSED IN LEMON JUICE, SO IF YOU WANT TO MAKE THIS IN ADVANCE, MIX ALL THE VEGGIES AND DRESSING TOGETHER, THEN PREPARE AND ADD THE AVOCADO AT THE LAST MINUTE. WE PREFER CHUNKY DICED AVOCADO TO THE MORE USUAL MASHED VERSION AND WE HOPE YOU DO, TOO.

Put the avocados, tomatoes, red bell pepper, red onion, and scallions into a bowl. Sprinkle with the parsley and gently toss together. Drizzle the oil and lemon juice over the salad, season to taste, then gently toss together. Serve immediately. We like it on a bed of Hummus, sprinkled with a little paprika and extra chopped fresh parsley.

TZATZIKI

1 cucumber
¼ teaspoon sea salt
1 cup (9oz/250g) Greek yogurt
1 garlic clove, crushed
freshly ground black pepper
olive oil, for drizzling

PRONOUNCED "DZA-DZI-KI," THIS IS WONDERFULLY COOLING AND REFRESHING, AND IS A GREAT ADDED EXTRA TO WRAPS, OR TO TOP SPICED MEATS OR VEGETABLES. SALTING THE CUCUMBER IS A NATURAL WAY TO MAKE SURE THERE'S ENOUGH (BUT NOT TOO MUCH) SALT IN THE DISH. THE SALTED CUCUMBER "SWEATS" OUT EXCESS SALT AND WATER, LEAVING YOU WITH A GREAT SALTY CUCUMBER FLESH AND AS LITTLE LIQUID AS POSSIBLE. THE DIP KEEPS FOR 3-4 DAYS IN THE REFRIGERATOR.

SERVES 6
MAKES: 2 CUPS (1LB 2OZ/500G)
PREP: 10 MINUTES
STAND: 30 MINUTES-
1 HOUR

1 Cut the cucumber in half lengthwise, then scoop out the seeds with a teaspoon. Finely chop the flesh, then put into a strainer and set this over a bowl. Sprinkle the salt over the cucumber and let stand for 30 minutes-1 hour to allow for the salt to draw out some of the juices and to drain into the bowl.

2 Put the yogurt, garlic, and a little black pepper into a mixing bowl and stir together. Add the cucumber, mix together, then spoon into a serving dish. Drizzle a little olive oil on top to serve.

TOMATO & CILANTRO SALSA

1 red onion, quartered

½–1 large green chili, quartered and seeded

½ cup (1oz/25g) chopped fresh cilantro

2 ripe tomatoes (about 9oz/250g), quartered, seeded, and chopped finely

2 tablespoons olive oil

sea salt and freshly ground black pepper

SERVES 6
MAKES: ABOUT 2 CUPS (ILB/450G)
PREP: IO MINUTES

HOW HOT YOU MAKE THIS IS VERY MUCH DOWN TO YOU AND THE KIND OF CHILIS THAT YOU USE. WE PREFER TO BUY THE LARGE FINGER CHILIS AND TO TAKE THE SEEDS OUT. START WITH HALF A CHOPPED CHILI, BECAUSE YOU CAN ALWAYS ADD EXTRA IF YOU WANT TO CRANK THE HEAT UP A LITTLE.

1 Put the onion, half the green chili, and the cilantro into a food processor and finely chop. Spoon into a serving bowl. Add the chopped tomatoes, then stir in the oil, ¼ teaspoon salt, and black pepper to taste. Alternatively, finely chop all the vegetables on a cutting board and mix with the salt, black pepper, and oil in a bowl.

2 Taste the salsa and gradually stir in the remaining chili, finely chopped, as needed. This will keep for 2–3 days in the refrigerator.

GREEN CHILI SAUCE

3 large long green chilis (abuot 4oz/115g), halved, seeded, and cut into chunks

2 plum tomatoes, peeled if desired and cut into chunks

½ cup (1oz/25g) fresh cilantro, including the leaves and stems

4 large garlic cloves, sliced

1 teaspoon coriander seeds, coarsely crushed

2 teaspoons granulated sugar

¼ teaspoon sea salt and freshly ground black pepper

SERVES 4–6
MAKES: ABOUT 1 CUP
(9FL OZ/250ML)
PREP: 10 MINUTES

DON'T THINK YOU'RE WIMPING OUT BY TAKING OUT THE CHILI SEEDS—THIS SAUCE IS PLENTY HOT WITHOUT THEM. OF COURSE, IF YOUR CHILIS ARE MILD, THEN LEAVE THE SEEDS IN. ADD JUST A TEASPOON OR TWO OF THIS TO ANY DISH, BUT IT'S ESPECIALLY NICE WITH BARBECUED EGGPLANTS, TAHINI SAUCE, AND HUMMUS—IT'S SMOKIN! FOR BEST RESULTS, ALWAYS ENHACE WITH A LITTLE LEMON JUICE JUST BEFORE SERVING.

Put all the ingredients into a blender or food processor and process until a coarse paste forms. Spoon into a screw-top jar or sealed container and store in the refrigerator. It will keep for at least a week.

YELLOW SAUCE

1 large garlic bulb (about 2½oz/70 g),
separated into cloves, smashed with
a knife, peeled, and halved

⅔ cup (5fl oz/150ml) olive oil

3 fresh thyme sprigs, leaves only,
to provide about 1 tablespoon

2 fresh sage sprigs, leaves only

⅓ cup (3oz/85g) granulated sugar

juice of 1 lemon

sea salt and freshly ground
black pepper

SERVES 6
MAKES: ¾ CUP (6FL OZ/175ML)
PREP: 10 MINUTES
COOK: 5 MINUTES

THIS SAUCE IS SERIOUSLY GARLICKY, SO A LITTLE GOES A
LONG WAY. ALTHOUGH IT'S GARLICKY, IT IS TEMPERED WITH
THE SWEET-AND-SOUR BALANCE OF SUGAR AND LEMON JUICE
AND IS SPECKLED GREEN WITH FRESH THYME AND SAGE
LEAVES. IT COMPLEMENTS THE ROASTED VEGETABLE SALAD
ON P. 84. ANY LEFTOVERS CAN BE KEPT IN A SCREW-TOP JAR
IN THE REFRIGERATOR AND CAN BE USED AS AN EASY SALAD
DRESSING OR TO LIFT BRUSCHETTA-STYLE BROILED TOMATOES
ON TOASTED CIABATTA OR SOURDOUGH FOR A QUICK LUNCH.

1 Put the garlic into a small saucepan, pour in half the oil, and cook over low heat for 5 minutes until the garlic is just turning pale golden brown. Remove from the heat, add the herbs, sugar, and lemon juice, and stir until the sugar has dissolved.

2 Transfer to a blender or a small food processor and process until smooth. Alternatively, use an immersion blender in the pan. Stir in the remaining oil and add salt and black pepper to taste.

3 Pour the sauce into a screw-top jar and screw on the lid. It will keep for 2–3 days in the refrigerator.

108

SERVES 4
MAKES ²/₃ CUP (5FL OZ/150ML)
PREP: 5 MINUTES
STAND: 30 MINUTES

GARLIC & LEMON SAUCE

juice of 3 lemons
3 garlic cloves, minced
2 pickled chili peppers, drained and finely chopped
sea salt and freshly ground black pepper

To serve:
Hummus (see p. 19)
warm Whole Wheat Pita Breads (see p. 110)

THIS IS A MIXTURE THAT ADDS A DIFFERENT DIMENSION TO ANY HUMMUS DISH. WE DON'T PUT GARLIC IN OUR HUMMUS (SOME CUSTOMERS DON'T WANT GARLIC BREATH, SO THIS GIVES THEM AN OPTION) BUT WE LOVE DRIZZLING THIS SAUCE OVER THE TOP—THE ACID FROM THE LEMONS TOGETHER WITH THE BITTERNESS OF THE GARLIC AND SPICED SALTINESS OF THE PICKLED CHILIS MAKE IT IRRESISTIBLE.

1 Put all the ingredients into a bowl and, using a fork, stir together to mix. Alternatively, put into a screw-top jar, screw on the lid, and shake well.

2 Let stand for 30 minutes or so for the flavors to develop, then strain. Drizzle over plates of Hummus and serve with warm Pita Breads.

COOK'S TIP

SAVE TIME AND AVOID GARLIC-SCENTED FINGERS BY PROCESSING ALL THE SAUCE INGREDIENTS TOGETHER IN A FOOD PROCESSOR INSTEAD OF CHOPPING BY HAND.

WHOLE WHEAT PITA BREAD

1 cup plus 3 tablespoons (5oz/140g) whole wheat flour

2 cups (9oz/250g) white bread flour, plus extra for dusting

1 teaspoon sea salt

1 teaspoon superfine or granulated sugar

2 teaspoons active dry yeast

1 cup (8fl oz/240ml) warm water

oil, for oiling

ACTIVE DRY YEAST MAKES BAKING BREAD SUPER-EASY, BECAUSE THERE'S NO WAITING AND FROTHING OF YEAST. JUST STIR IT INTO THE FLOUR WITH THE WARM WATER AND GET GOING. THE OVEN TEMPERATURE MIGHT SEEM LOWER THAN FOR MOST BREADS, BUT IT REALLY DOES WORK. IF YOU HAVE A GLASS OVEN DOOR, THE KIDS WILL LOVE TO WATCH THE BREADS PUFF UP MAGICALLY IN THE OVEN.

1 Put the flours, salt, and sugar into an electric mixer, then sprinkle the yeast over the top and stir together. With the machine running, gradually mix in enough of the warm water until a soft dough is formed, then beat for 5 minutes on low speed.

2 Increase the machine speed and mix for another 5 minutes to develop the gluten and until the dough is silky smooth and elastic. If you don't have a mixer, then make the dough in a bowl with a wooden spoon and knead on a lightly floured work surface for as long as your muscles will let you.

3 Transfer the dough to a lightly oiled bowl, cover the top with oiled plastic wrap, and put in a warm place for 30 minutes until the dough is almost twice the size.

4 Knead the dough once again, but this time just for a few minutes. Cut into eight pieces, then roll out each piece to a circle 5–6 inches (13–15cm) in diameter. Place on lightly floured baking sheets and cover once again with oiled plastic wrap. Let rise for 30 minutes. Meanwhile, preheat the oven to (350°F) 180°C.

5 Remove the plastic wrap and bake the breads for 3–5 minutes until puffed up and just beginning to tinge brown. Remove and wrap in a clean dish towel to keep them soft. Serve warm, split and filled, or reheat cold Pita Breads on a preheated ridged grill pan for 2–3 minutes or under a hot broiler.

MAKES 8
PREP: 25 MINUTES
RISE: 1 HOUR
COOK: 3–5 MINUTES

FLATBREAD WITH ZA'ATAR

4 cups (1lb 2oz/500g) white bread flour, plus a little extra for dusting

1 teaspoon salt

2 teaspoons active dry yeast

2 teaspoons honey

¼ cup (2fl oz/60ml) olive oil, plus extra for oiling and drizzling

1¼ cups (10fl oz/300ml) warm water

1 tablespoon Za'atar Spice Blend (see p. 92)

2 tablespoons sesame seeds

MAKES: 2 LARGE BREADS
PREP: 30 MINUTES
RISE: 1½ HOURS
COOK: 15–20 MINUTES

VERSIONS OF THIS FLATBREAD CAN BE FOUND ALL OVER THE MIDDLE EAST AND SERVED FOR BREAKFAST OR AS PART OF A MEZZE. BREAK THROUGH THE FRAGRANT CRISP ZA'ATAR AND SESAME CRUST TO THE SOFT DOUGH BENEATH. MAKING YOUR OWN BREAD IS WONDERFULLY RELAXING, BUT THE HARDEST PART IS WAITING FOR IT TO BE COOL ENOUGH TO EAT!

1 Put the flour, salt, and yeast into a large mixing bowl and stir together. Add the honey and 2 tablespoons of the oil and gradually mix in enough warm water with a wooden spoon, then mix with your hands to make a soft but not sticky dough. You may not need all of the water.

2 Knead the dough for 5 minutes until smooth and elastic. Alternatively, mix and knead in an electric mixer with a dough hook, if you have one.

3 Put the dough into a large, lightly oiled bowl, cover with oiled plastic wrap, and let rise in a warm place for 45–60 minutes, or until the dough has doubled in size.

4 Punch the dough down with a fist, then scoop out of the bowl and knead well on a lightly floured work surface for

2–3 minutes until smooth again. Cut the dough in half and roll each half out to a circle about 9 inches (23cm) in diameter. Put each onto an oiled baking sheet.

5 Slash the top of each bread with crisscross lines, brush with the remaining oil, then sprinkle with the za'atar and sesame seeds. Cover the top of each bread loosely with oiled plastic wrap and let rise for 30 minutes. Meanwhile, preheat the oven to 425°F (230°C).

6 Remove the plastic wrap and bake the breads for 15–20 minutes, swapping oven positions around after 10 minutes so that they brown evenly. Cook until golden brown and the bread sounds hollow when tapped with your fingertips. Drizzle with a little extra olive oil. Transfer to a wire rack to cool, then break into pieces to serve.

COOK'S TIP

IF YOU DON'T THINK YOU WILL BE ABLE TO EAT BOTH BREADS, THEN WRAP ONE IN PLASTIC WRAP WHEN COMPLETELY COLD, SEAL, LABEL, AND FREEZE FOR UP TO A MONTH. DEFROST AT ROOM TEMPERATURE, THEN UNWRAP AND WARM IN A LOW OVEN BEFORE SERVING.

LABANEH
(SOUR YOGURT CHEESE)

6½ cups (3¼lb/1.5kg)
plain whole yogurt

1 teaspoon fine grain salt

To serve:
olive oil, for drizzling
Za'atar Spice Blend (see p. 92)
warm Whole Wheat Pita Breads
(see p. 110)

RONEN: I LOVE TO EAT LABANEH SPREAD ON PAPER-THIN DRUZE PITA BREAD WITH ZA'ATAR AND PICKLED OREGANO LEAVES. MY SISTER'S GIRLS ARE ALSO HUGE FANS—A SANDWICH WITH LABANEH IS THEIR PREFERRED LUNCH ALL WEEK LONG.

IT'S THE ULTIMATE SIMPLE FOOD BECAUSE IT'S EASY TO MAKE AND EFFORTLESS TO SERVE. SIMPLY STIR SOME SALT INTO YOGURT AND LET DRIP, TIED IN CHEESECLOTH, FOR 8-12 HOURS OR OVERNIGHT. IF YOU TIE THE BAG OVER THE FAUCET BEFORE YOU GO TO BED, THE YOGURT CAN DRIP STRAIGHT INTO THE SINK, THEN TRANSFER IT TO THE REFRIGERATOR THE NEXT MORNING. THE LONGER YOU LEAVE IT, THE DENSER THE CHEESE WILL BE.

LABANEH IS IDEAL AS PART OF A MEZZE. IT CAN ALSO BE SHAPED INTO SMALL BALLS AND KEPT IN A JAR OF OLIVE OIL TO PROLONG ITS KEEPING.

SERVES 8-10
MAKES 1¼LB (550G)
PREP: 10 MINUTES
STAND: 8-12 HOURS
OR OVERNIGHT

1 Put a large square of cheesecloth that is at least 15 inches (38cm) square into a mixing bowl. Pour boiling water over it and let soak for 3-4 minutes to sterilize it. Remove with tongs, then drape the cloth over a colander set over a second smaller bowl.

2 Drain the water from the bowl, dry, and add the yogurt and salt. Stir together, then spoon into the cheesecloth-lined colander. Bring the edges of the cloth together over the yogurt, twist, and tie with string and make a loop long enough to hook over the kitchen faucet.

Or tie it from the knob of a high kitchen cabinet door or use a preserving jelly stand, if you have one. Make sure you have a bowl under the bag to catch the liquid; it will run out quickly and look white and milky to begin with, then after 10 minutes will begin to drip clear liquid. Let hang for 8-12 hours or overnight until firm.

3 Transfer the cloth bag of cheese to a plate. Chill in the refrigerator until required, then peel away the cloth, put on a board, and serve drizzled with olive oil and za'atar spice mix with warm Pita Breads as part of a mezze-style mix of dishes.

COOK'S TIP

DON'T BE TEMPTED TO USE FAT-FREE YOGURT BECAUSE YOU NEED THE FAT FOR THE BEST FLAVOR.

DESSERTS

MALABI

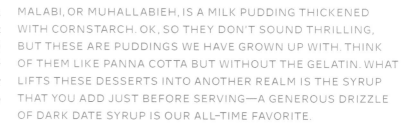

scant ½ cup (2oz/55g) cornstarch
2½ cups (1 pint/600ml) whole milk
scant ½ cup (3½fl oz/100ml) heavy cream
½ cup (3½oz/100g) granulated sugar
3 tablespoons date syrup

To decorate:
fresh baby mint leaves
pomegranate seeds (optional)

SERVES 6
PREP: 10 MINUTES
COOK: 5 MINUTES
SET: 3–4 HOURS

MALABI, OR MUHALLABIEH, IS A MILK PUDDING THICKENED WITH CORNSTARCH. OK, SO THEY DON'T SOUND THRILLING, BUT THESE ARE PUDDINGS WE HAVE GROWN UP WITH. THINK OF THEM LIKE PANNA COTTA BUT WITHOUT THE GELATIN. WHAT LIFTS THESE DESSERTS INTO ANOTHER REALM IS THE SYRUP THAT YOU ADD JUST BEFORE SERVING—A GENEROUS DRIZZLE OF DARK DATE SYRUP IS OUR ALL-TIME FAVORITE.

1 Put the cornstarch into a bowl and gradually mix in about one-third of the milk to make a smooth paste.

2 Pour the rest of the milk into a medium saucepan, add the cream and sugar, and heat gently so that the sugar dissolves. When the creamy milk mixture begins to get hot and release steam, gradually stir in the cornstarch paste with a wooden spoon. Continue heating the milk mix until it is brought to a boil. Check the temperature with a candy thermometer. As soon as it reaches 203°F (95°C), the mix will begin to thicken. Remove from the heat immediately.

3 Pour into six damp ⅔-cup (5fl-oz/150-ml) individual ramekins or dessert molds and let cool at room temperature. Cover the tops with plastic wrap and chill in the refrigerator for 3 hours, longer if you have the time, so that the puddings can set firm.

4 When you are ready to serve, loosen the edges of the malabi with a damp knife, then turn them out onto small curved plates. Drizzle the date syrup over the puddings and decorate with fresh mint leaves and pomegranate seeds.

SERVES 6
PREP: 15 MINUTES
COOK: 16–18 MINUTES

GLUTEN-FREE CHOCOLATE BROWNIES

3 tablespoons (1½oz/40g) butter, plus extra for greasing

10oz (300g) semisweet chocolate, broken into pieces

scant ½ cup (6oz/175g) granulated sugar

⅔ cup (5fl oz/150ml) heavy cream

3 eggs, separated

To serve:

sifted confectioners' sugar

few sliced pistachio nuts

salted cashew or vanilla ice cream (optional)

IT'S HARD TO RESIST THESE DARK, RICH, CHOCOLATE-PACKED BROWNIES WITH THEIR SOFT GOOEY CENTERS. SERVE WHILE WARM FROM THE OVEN OR LET THEM COOL COMPLETELY AND TOP WITH A SCOOP OF GOOD VANILLA ICE CREAM OR A SPOONFUL OF GREEK YOGURT FLAVORED WITH A LITTLE GROUND CINNAMON AND HONEY. WHICHEVER WAY YOU CHOOSE, THEY MAKE A FABULOUS FINALE TO A DINNER SHARED WITH FRIENDS.

1 Preheat the oven to 275°F (140°C). Grease the inside of six individual ceramic or foil dishes that are 4 inches (10cm) in diameter and 1½ inches (4cm) deep. Set them on a baking sheet.

2 Put the butter, chocolate, and granulated sugar into a large, heatproof bowl. Pour in the cream and set the bowl over a saucepan of gently simmering water, making sure that the water does not touch the bottom of the bowl. Heat for about 5 minutes, stirring gently from time to time, until the chocolate has completely melted and the mixture is smooth and glossy.

3 Remove the bowl from the heat, and gradually stir in the egg yolks, one by one, until smooth. Whisk the egg whites in a separate bowl until a thick foam forms that softly peaks when the beaters are lifted out of the mixture. Add to the chocolate and gently fold together with a large metal or silicone spoon.

4 Spoon the chocolate batter evenly into the dishes and bake for 16–18 minutes until the tops are dry to the touch, the mixture is set around the edges, and the center still has a soft slight wobble. Let stand for 10–15 minutes, then dust with sifted confectioners' sugar, sprinkle with sliced pistachios, and serve warm or cold. A scoop of salted cashew or vanilla ice cream on the side is also good.

HALVAH PARFAIT

6 extra-large eggs, separated

heaped ½ cup (4oz/115g) granulated sugar

1¾ cups (14fl oz/400ml) whipping cream

½ (1-lb/450-g) package plain halvah, sliced and broken into small pieces

fresh figs or sliced peaches, to serve (optional)

SERVES 6–8
PREP: 20 MINUTES
FREEZE: 6–8 HOURS
OR OVERNIGHT

COULDN'T BE SIMPLER. IF YOU HAVEN'T BOUGHT HALVAH BEFORE, IT IS MADE WITH TAHINI, SUGAR, AND SOMETIMES VANILLA AND IS SOLD IN I-POUND (450-G) PACKAGES OR IN SMALLER BARS, EITHER PLAIN OR FLAVORED. IT HAS A TEXTURE A LITTLE LIKE SPONGE CANDY (HONEYCOMB TOFFEE). ALTHOUGH YOU CAN SLICE IT, HALVAH BREAKS AND CRUMBLES AS SOON AS YOU TOUCH IT WITH A KNIFE. SCRUNCH UP ANY BIGGER PIECES WITH YOUR FINGERS. UNLIKE OTHER HOMEMADE ICE CREAM, THIS IS EASY TO SLICE STRAIGHT FROM THE FREEZER. THANK YOU, ANAT, FOR GIVING US THIS RECIPE MANY YEARS AGO.

1 Put the egg whites and 2 teaspoons of the sugar into one large bowl and the egg yolks and the remaining sugar into another large bowl. Using an electric mixer, whisk the egg whites and sugar until thick moist-looking peaks that hold their shape when the beaters are lifted above the mixture form.

2 There's no need to wash the beaters—quickly use them to whisk the egg yolks and sugar together for 3–4 minutes until thick and pale. Now, use the eletric mixer to whip the cream in a smaller bowl until it forms soft swirls.

3 Fold the cream into the egg yolk mix, then fold in the crumbled halvah. Gently fold in the egg whites until no white lumps remain. Pour the mixture into a 2½-quart (2.5-liter) small roasting pan. If you don't have one that kind of size, a disposable foil roasting dish, about 7 x 10 x 2½ inches (18 x 25 x 6cm) works well, or use a large loaf pan or large plastic container. Cover with plastic wrap or a lid and freeze for 6-8 hours or overnight until firm.

4 Cut into thick slices to serve. It is delicious served on its own or with fresh figs or sliced peaches.

SERVES 6
PREP: 5 MINUTES
COOK: 55 MINUTES

ORANGE BLOSSOM RICE PUDDING

4¼ cups (1¾ pints/1 liter) water
1 cup (7oz/200g) risotto rice
2 cups (18fl oz/500ml) cold whole milk
¾ cup (5oz/150g) granulated sugar
⅔ cup (5fl oz/150ml) heavy cream
½ teaspoon orange blossom water, plus extra for sprinkling (optional)

To decorate:
chopped Turkish delight
chopped pistachios
plus a few sliced pistachios

RONEN: THIS IS MY SISTER'S RECIPE. FORGET ABOUT RICE PUDDING SERVED AT SCHOOL— THIS CREAMY, SMOOTH VERSION IS MADE WITH RISOTTO RICE GENTLY COOKED ON THE STOVE AND THEN FINISHED WITH HEAVY CREAM, SUGAR, AND JUST A HINT OF EXOTICALLY FRAGRANT ORANGE BLOSSOM WATER. IT'S WONDERFUL SERVED COLD, DRIZZLED WITH A LITTLE EXTRA CREAM AND SPRINKLED WITH SOME CHOPPED TURKISH DELIGHT AND PISTACHIOS, BUT IT IS JUST AS DELICIOUS SERVED AS SOON AS IT HAS BEEN MADE, SPRINKLED WITH A LITTLE GROUND CINNAMON.

1 Pour the water into a saucepan, bring to a boil, and then add the risotto rice. Bring the water back to a boil, then lower the heat and simmer gently for 15 minutes until the rice is beginning to soften and looks a little like porridge. Stir from time so that the rice doesn't stick to the pan.

2 Stir in the cold milk and bring to a boil, then lower the heat and simmer for about 40 minutes, stirring from time to time, until the rice is thick and creamy and nearly all the milk and water have been absorbed by the rice. Make sure to stir more often, the thicker the rice gets.

3 Add the sugar and cook over low heat, stirring frequently, until the sugar has dissolved. Mix in the cream and cook for another 5 minutes until the rice is soft. Stir in the orange flower water, then let cool slightly. Taste. If the orange flavor is too subtle, you can add a little more orange blossom water.

4 Spoon into bowls or let cool completely. Serve, sprinkled with a little chopped Turkish delight, chopped and sliced pistachios, and a little extra orange blossom water, if desired.

PANNA COTTA WITH ROSE WATER

5 sheets (¼oz/7g) gelatin
2 cups (¾ pint/450ml) heavy cream
⅔ cup (5fl oz/150ml) lowfat milk
3 tablespoons honey
few drops of rose water, or to taste

To decorate:
tiny pale pink rose petals (optional)
chopped Turkish delight (optional)

SERVES 6
PREP: 15 MINUTES
SET: 4–5 HOURS

COOK'S TIP

ROSE WATER VARIES IN STRENGTH, SO ADD JUST A FEW DROPS, THEN TASTE AND ADD MORE, IF NEEDED. YOU MIGHT ALSO WANT TO TRY ADDING A LITTLE ROSE WATER TO SOME WHIPPED CREAM—GREAT WITH OUR CHOCOLATE BROWNIES (SEE P. 120).

WE HAVE GIVEN THE CLASSIC ITALIAN DESSERT OUR OWN MIDDLE EASTERN TWIST. JUST A DASH OF ROSE WATER ADDS AN EXOTIC PERFUME, AND SERVED WITH PASTEL PINK ROSE PETALS, MAKES THIS A LIGHT FINALE TO A SPECIAL MEAL.

1 Separate the gelatin sheets and put into a shallow bowl, just cover with cold water, and let soak for 5 minutes.

2 Pour the cream and milk into a saucepan, add the honey, and bring just to a boil, stirring, until the honey has dissolved. Drain the water from the gelatin, then add the softened sheets to the hot cream mixture after removing it from the heat, and stir until they have dissolved.

3 Stir in a few drops of rose water, taste, and add a few more drops, if desired. Pour the cream mixture into six ⅔-cup (5-fl oz/150-ml) dessert molds or ramekins and let cool, then chill in the refrigerator for 4–5 hours until set.

4 To serve, leave the desserts in the molds or turn out by dipping each mold into hot water for 10 seconds, loosen the top of the dessert with your fingertips, then invert onto a plate. Holding the mold and plate, jerk to release the panna cotta. Remove the molds and decorate the desserts with a few tiny pink rose petals, if desired, or chopped Turkish delight.

MINT & GINGER LEMONADE

¾ cup (5½oz/150g) granulated sugar

⅔ cup (5fl oz/150ml) water

2-inch (5-cm) piece fresh ginger, scrubbed (there's no need to peel), sliced

juice of 8 lemons

To serve:

chilled water and ice cubes

6 fresh mint sprigs

wafer-thin strips of fresh ginger, cut with a vegetable peeler (optional)

MAKES: 6 GLASSES
PREP: 10 MINUTES
COOK: 5 MINUTES
CHILL: 2–3 HOURS

EASY TO MAKE AND REALLY REFRESHING ON A HOT SUMMERY DAY, THIS DRINK IS GREAT FOR PARTIES, TOO. JUST SCALE UP THE QUANTITIES—AND FOR THOSE WHO LIKE AN EXTRA HIT, TRY IT WITH A SPLASH OF WHITE RUM.

1 Put the sugar, water, and ginger into a small saucepan and heat over low heat, stirring until the sugar has dissolved. Bring to a boil, then remove from the heat, cover with a lid or plate, and let cool at room temperature for 2–3 hours for the flavors to develop.

2 Strain the lemon juice into a liquid measuring cup; you should have about 1¾ cups (15fl oz/400ml). Strain in the ginger syrup and stir to mix, then top up to 7 cups (3 pints/1.7 liters) with chilled water and ice cubes. Stir together, then pour into six glasses and add a mint sprig and strip of ginger, if using, to each to serve.

HOT SPICED APPLE CIDER

2 teaspoons ground cinnamon
½ teaspoon grated nutmeg
¼ teaspoon ground cloves
¼ teaspoon ground ginger
5¼ cups (2 pints/1.25 liters)
apple cider

4 cinnamon sticks, to serve (optional)

NOT EVERYONE IS A FAN OF TEA OR COFFEE, AND THIS
WARMING CAFFEINE-FREE DRINK WILL SOON HELP YOU
TO THAW OUT ON A COLD WINTER'S DAY.

1 Mix all the ground spices together in a small bowl (make sure there are no lumps), then divide among four mugs or heavy, heatproof glasses.

2 Pour the apple cider into a saucepan and gently warm over low heat, making sure that you don't boil it. Pour into the mugs and stir the cider and spices together with cinnamon sticks or teaspoons, if you prefer, and serve immediately.

MAKES 4 MUGS
OR GLASSES
PREP: 2 MINUTES
COOK: 2–3 MINUTES

CARDAMOM COFFEE

1 cardamom pod
1 cup (8fl oz/240ml) cold water
1–2 teaspoons granulated sugar,
or to taste
1 tablespoon finely ground coffee

WARM, FRAGRANT, AND WONDERFULLY EXOTIC, TURKISH COFFEE WITH A TWIST, THIS IS TRADITIONALLY MADE IN AN *IBRIK* (*BRIKI* IN GREEK), A SMALL METAL JUGLIKE SAUCEPAN WITH A LONG HANDLE. DON'T WORRY IF DON'T HAVE ONE, BECAUSE A SMALL SAUCEPAN WILL WORK JUST AS WELL. IT'S VITAL TO HAVE THE COFFEE GROUND FINELY UNTIL IT IS ALMOST LIKE POWDER. YOU CAN DO THIS AT HOME IN A SPICE MILL OR POWERFUL BLENDER, OR ASK THE DELI TO GRIND THE COFFEE FOR "TURKISH COFFEE."

1 Put the cardamom pod in a mortar and crush with the pestle, then remove the seeds and grind them finely.

2 Pour the water into an ibrik or small saucepan, add enough sugar to taste, then heat until the sugar has dissolved. Bring just to a boil, then remove from the heat and add the ground coffee, empty cardamom pod, and the ground seeds.

3 Bring the water gently to a boil again, then remove from the heat as soon as the coffee begins to foam. Let cool for 1–2 minutes, then put back on the heat and return to a boil so that the coffee is foaming. Pour into a coffee cup. Scoop out the cardamom pod, which will have floated to the surface, with a teaspoon. Let stand for 1–2 minutes for the coffee grounds to settle. Don't be tempted to stir the coffee or add milk or cream. Serve.

MAKES: 1 CUP
PREP AND COOK:
5 MINUTES

MINT & SAGE TEAS

24 fresh mint sprigs (about 1oz/30g)

3½ cups (1½ pints/840ml) boiling water

sugar or honey, to taste (optional)

POPULAR SINCE ROMAN TIMES, MINT TEA IS STILL WIDELY DRUNK IN MIDDLE EASTERN CAFES AND HOMES. THE SCENT AND TASTE OF MINT IS THOUGHT TO IMPROVE A PERSON'S MOOD AND TO AID RELAXATION, WHILE ALSO ACTING AS A REFRESHING DIGESTIVE AND STOMACH SOOTHER.

Put the mint into a teapot or heatproof liquid measuring cup, pour the boiling water over it, cover with a lid or saucer, and let brew for 4–5 minutes until the water is pale green. Strain the tea into four heatproof glasses, then scoop out some of the mint from the measuring cup and add a sprig to each glass. We prefer to serve it just as it is, but if you have a sweet tooth, stir in a little sugar or honey to taste.

MAKES: 4 GLASSES
PREP: 5 MINUTES

SAGE TEA

People have been cooking with sage since the fifth century BC. The Arabs used to associate it with immortality, while it's botanical name *Salvia* is from the Latin "to save" or "to heal." Herbalists once had a saying, "Why should anyone die with sage in their garden?" While we cannot vouch for its lifesaving properties, we do recommend it as a digestive, and as a soothing and calming caffeine-free pick-me-up. Make it in just the same way as mint tea and sweeten with a little honey, if desired.

SACHLAV

3 tablespoons cornstarch
2½ cups (1 pint/600ml) whole milk
⅔ cup (5fl oz/150ml) heavy cream
⅓ cup (3oz/85g) granulated sugar

To serve:
ground cinnamon
chopped peanuts and/or pistachios
coconut shavings

SERVES 4
PREP: 5 MINUTES
COOK: 4–5 MINUTES

TRADITIONALLY SERVED WARM FROM STREET VENDORS, THIS COMFORTING MILKY DRINK ALWAYS REMINDS US OF CHILDHOOD. DUST A GENEROUS AMOUNT OF GROUND CINNAMON OVER THE SURFACE WITH A SMALL TEA STRAINER, AND TOP WITH CHOPPED PEANUTS, PISTACHIOS, AND COCONUT SHAVINGS. IF IT IS ESPECIALLY THICK, IT CAN SOMETIMES BE HARD TO DRINK, SO IT IS WORTH GIVING GUESTS A SMALL TEASPOON TO SCOOP IT UP.

1 Put the cornstarch into a saucepan, mix in a little of the milk to make a smooth paste, then add the remaining milk, cream, and sugar. Bring to a boil over medium heat, stirring until slightly thickened.

2 As soon as the mixture has thickened, remove from the heat, pour into heatproof glasses, and top with the ground cinnamon, chopped nuts, and coconut shavings to serve.

NOTE

SACHLAV IS THE ARABIC AND HEBREW NAME FOR "ORCHID," AND THIS DRINK WAS ORIGINALLY THICKENED WITH GROUND ORCHID ROOT, ALTHOUGH CORNSTARCH, A MORE ACCESSIBLE EVERYDAY THICKENER, IS USED NOW.

OUZO & GRAPEFRUIT SLUSH

5 ruby grapefruits, freshly squeezed or 4¼ cups (1¾ pints/1 liter) prepared chilled ruby grapefruit juice

½ cup (4fl oz/125ml) ouzo

¼ cup (½oz/15g) chopped fresh mint

SLUSH PUPPIES FOR ADULTS! QUICK AND EASY TO MIX TOGETHER, THEN FREEZE IN A SHALLOW CONTAINER— THE LARGER THE PAN, THE THINNER THE MIXTURE WILL BE AND THE QUICKER IT WILL FREEZE. THE SECRET IS TO BREAK UP THE ICE WITH A FORK AT REGULAR INTERVALS SO THAT THE MIXTURE BECOMES LIKE FINE SNOW. SERVE IN SMALL GLASSES WITH A TEASPOON OR STRAWS. IF YOU ARE SQUEEZING YOUR OWN JUICE, KEEP THE GRAPEFRUIT SHELLS TO USE AS FUN SERVING DISHES.

SERVES 4
PREP: 15 MINUTES
FREEZE: 3 HOURS

1 Pour the grapefruit juice and ouzo into a large cake pan or roasting pan and mix together. Cover the top with plastic wrap and put into the coldest part of the freezer. Freeze for 1 hour.

2 Take the pan out of the freezer and break up the ice with a fork. Return to the freezer and freeze for 2 hours, breaking up with a fork at 30–45 minute intervals, until the mixture looks like fine snow.

3 Beat in the chopped mint and transfer to a plastic container, press a lid in place, and freeze until needed. Break up with a fork just before serving, scooped into grapefruit shells or glasses with little straws.

COOK'S TIP

YOU MIGHT ALSO WANT TO TRY WITH ORANGE JUICE AND TEQUILA, FRESH LEMONADE AND GIN, OR FROZEN CARDAMOM COFFEE VERSIONS.

QUICK SNACKS

HALVAH COOKIES

7 tablespoons (3½oz/100g) unsalted butter, at room temperature

⅓ cup (3oz/85g) superfine or granulated sugar

⅓ cup (3oz/85g) tahini

½ teaspoon vanilla extract

1 teaspoon baking powder

1 cup plus 3 tablespoons (5½oz/150g) all-purpose flour

MAKES 15
PREP: 15 MINUTES
COOK: 8–10 MINUTES

THESE CRUMBLY SHORTBREADLIKE COOKIES JUST MELT IN THE MOUTH. THEY TAKE ONLY A FEW MINUTES TO MAKE AND BAKE. HOWEVER, THE BAKING PROCESS IS CRITICAL, SO DON'T LEAVE THE KITCHEN WHILE THEY ARE BAKING; YOU NEED TO CATCH THEM WHEN THEY ARE LIGHT GOLDEN, NO MORE THAN THAT. IF YOU OVERCOOK THEM, THE COOKIES WILL TAKE ON A SOUR, ALMOST BITTER, TASTE.

1 Preheat the oven to 350°F (180°C) and line two baking sheets with parchment paper.

2 Cream the butter and sugar together in a bowl with a wooden spoon or beat in a food processor until light and fluffy.

3 Add the tahini and vanilla and beat together until smooth again. Add the baking powder and flour to another bowl and stir together, then gradually beat into the creamed tahini mixture, pressing together with your hands to make a ball when it is too stiff to mix.

4 Scoop the dough into 15 mounds, then roll each one into a ball and put on the lined baking sheet, leaving a little space between them to spread during baking. Gently flatten the balls with a fork, then bake for 8–10 minutes until the tops have cracked and the cookies are pale golden. Let the cookies cool and harden on the paper. If you eat them while they are still warm, they will just crumble.

MORNING GRANOLA

2½ cups (9oz/250g) rolled oats
⅓ cup (2oz/55g) pumpkin seeds
⅓ cup (2oz/55g) sunflower seeds
½ cup (2oz/55g) slivered almonds
⅓ cup (1½oz/40g) pistachio nuts, sliced
2 tablespoons dried coconut
2 tablespoons sesame seeds
¼ cup (2fl oz/60ml) vegetable oil
½ cup (4fl oz/120ml) date syrup
1½ teaspoons ground cinnamon
pinch of sea salt
½ cup (2½oz/70g) dried cranberries
diced or sliced fruit and Greek yogurt or milk, to serve

SERVES 6
MAKES: 5⅓ CUPS (1½LB/650G)
PREP: 15 MINUTES
COOK: 30 MINUTES

DELICIOUSLY HEALTHY, THIS EASY BREAKFAST CEREAL IS NATURALLY SWEETENED WITH DATE SYRUP, ALSO CALLED DATE HONEY OR DATE MOLASSES—IT COMES IN JARS FROM THE HEALTH FOOD STORE OR ONLINE AND LOOKS A LITTLE LIKE MOLASSES. THIS GRANOLA IS PACKED WITH OATS FOR SLOW-RELEASE CARBS PLUS PROTEIN-RICH NUTS AND MINERAL-BOOSTING SEEDS TO POWER BOOST YOU UNTIL LUNCHTIME.

MAKE UP A BATCH OF THIS AT THE WEEKEND, BECAUSE YOU NEED TO BE IN THE KITCHEN TO STIR IT FREQUENTLY WHILE IT BAKES, THEN WHEN IT'S COLD, PACK IT INTO A STORAGE JAR. FABULOUS SERVED WITH SLICED BANANAS, DICED PEACHES, OR WHATEVER FRUIT YOU HAVE AVAILABLE, PLUS A GENEROUS SPOONFUL OF GREEK YOGURT, OR KEEP IT REALLY SIMPLE AND JUST DRIZZLE WITH SOME MILK.

1 Preheat the oven to 300°F (150°C).

2 Put all the ingredients except the cranberries into a bowl and mix together with a spoon to evenly coat the oats, nuts, and seeds with the oil and date syrup.

3 Transfer to a large roasting pan and press into an even layer, then bake for 30 minutes, stirring every 5-10 minutes so that the mixture doesn't form large, hard clumps. You will find that the granola in the corners will bake more quickly than that in the center, so keep a careful eye on it while it bakes and remember to set the timer so that you don't forget to keep stirring.

4 When the granola is crisp and a deep brown, remove from the oven and let cool, stirring every now and again to keep it from making large clumps. When cold, stir in the cranberries, then store in a large jar, screw on the lid, and keep in the refrigerator for up to a week. Serve with diced or sliced fruit and yogurt or milk.

TIP

IF YOU DON'T HAVE ALL THE NUTS OR ARE A LITTLE SHORT OF ONE INGREDIENT, THEN MIX AND MATCH WITH WHAT YOU DO HAVE. PECANS OR MACADAMIA NUTS ALSO TASTE GREAT.

SALT-PICKLED CUCUMBERS

146

2¼lb (1kg) fresh pickling cucumbers

5 garlic cloves

1–2 red chilis, split in half
(or a combination of
red and green chilis)

1 bunch of fresh dill

4¼ cups (1¾ pints/1 liter) water
(preferably mineral)

2 tablespoons kosher sea salt

2 tablespoons white wine vinegar

2 bay leaves

pinch of black peppercorns

1 tablespoon coriander seeds,
mustard seeds, or cumin seeds

MAKES: 2 JARS
PREP: 20 MINUTES
COOK: 1–2 WEEKS

CHOOSE THE FRESHEST AND SMALLEST HARD CUCUMBERS THAT YOU CAN FIND—IF YOU GROW PICKLING CUCUMBERS OR FIND THEM IN A FARMERS' MARKET, THESE ARE PERFECT. WE USE MINI CUCUMBERS SOLD BY SOME RETAILERS BECAUSE THEY DON'T CONTAIN AS MUCH WATER AS THE LARGE/LONG CUCUMBERS THAT ARE SOLD IN THE SUPERMARKETS.

1 Wash the cucumbers thoroughly in cold water. Place them in clean sterilized perserving jar(s) vertically, then put the garlic, chilis, and dill in between the cucumbers so they all "touch" each other.

2 The salt needs to dissolve in the water, so the easiest way is to boil the water with the salt and vinegar and let cool. When the water is at room temperature, add the bay leaves, peppercorns, and coriander, mustard, or cumin seeds. Add the water to the cucumbers, making sure that they are immersed in the water solution. If the jar you are using is not full, add more salty water: 4¼ cups (1¾ pints/1 liter) water to 2 tablespoons salt.

3 Close and seal the jar(s). To speed up the pickling process, you can put the jar(s) on the windowsill to catch the sunlight.

4 Taste the cucumbers every three days or so until they reach their required consistency. It should take 1–2 weeks. Keep in the refrigerator once you're happy with the taste. They should keep for a month if not contaminated.

148 # PICKLED LEMONS

4 fresh hard lemons (about 14oz/400g)
¼ cup (2oz/55g) kosher sea salt
2 tablespoons sunflower oil
½ green chili and ½ red chili,
coarsely chopped (optional)

THESE ARE SO VERSATILE: USE THEM FOR SALADS TO ADD ACIDITY, THEY'RE GREAT WITH BROILED CHICKEN, AND COMBINED WITH TAHINI SAUCE AND CHILI, THEY MAKE A GOOD DIP. YOU CAN ALSO INCLUDE SOME CHILIS TO ADD SOME SPICE TO THE LEMONS (SEE PHOTO ON P. 147).

1 Slice the lemons into thin slices. Place on a large baking sheet and sprinkle with the salt to make them "sweat." Let rest overnight, turning the slices once to make sure the salt reaches both sides.

2 Place the lemon slices, along with any liquid produced, in a clean, sterlized perserving jar and seal the lid. Let rest for 2–3 days for the lemons to sweat some more.

3 Add the oil until the lemons are covered and add the chilis, if desired.

4 Close the jar and place in a dark, dry place. Check the lemons every 2–3 days. They should be ready within 6–10 days and can last a few months.

MAKES: I JAR
PREP: IO MINUTES
STAND: 9–13 DAYS

SPICED FAVA BEAN NIBBLES

1½ cups (9oz/250g) dried fava beans or chickpeas, soaked overnight (or use canned, drained)

2 teaspoons baking soda

dash of olive oil

2 tablespoons dried oregano, plus extra for spinkling

sea salt and freshly ground black pepper

2 teaspoons garlic powder (optional)

2 teaspoons chili powder (optional)

SERVES: 4–6
PREP: OVERNIGHT
SOAK (OPTIONAL)
COOK: 1½ HOURS

THIS IS A CUTE AND FUN RECIPE THAT YOU CAN TRY WITH YOUR KIDS AT HOME. IT'S A PERFECT NIBBLE TO SERVE AT A FAMILY GATHERING. YOU CAN ALSO MAKE THIS WITH CHICKPEAS, BUT FAVA BEANS ARE MEATIER AND SOAK UP THE FLAVORS BETTER. CHILDREN LIKE THESE WITH OREGANO, OR MAYBE A LITTLE GARLIC POWDER. ADULTS TEND TO PREFER SOMETHING A LITTLE SPICIER, SO OMIT THE OREGANO AND REPLACE WITH CHILI POWDER.

1 Drain the soaked fava beans (or chickpeas), place in a saucepan with enough water to cover by about ¾ inch (2cm) and add the baking soda. Bring to a boil, then turn down the heat and cook for 45 minutes until they're soft enough to squash between two fingers (but still have shape). Drain in a strainer and then pat dry with paper towels (you want as little water as possible on the beans).

2 In a mixing bowl, add the herbs and/or spices, the beans, and the olive oil and mix well, being careful not to damage the beans. Season to taste.

3 Preheat the oven to 350°F (180°C). Spread the spiced beans over a baking sheet lined with parchment paper and bake for 40 minutes. After 20 minutes, remove the pan from the oven and give it a good shake to turn the beans. Return to the oven and repeat the process every 10 minutes. After 30 minutes, watch carefully because they can burn easily. After about 40 minutes, when the beans become brown and dry, remove from the oven. When cool enough to taste, check they are nice and crunchy on the outside.

4 Serve in a deep bowl with a sprinkle of salt crystals and a little extra oregano to enhance the flavor. Great with beer or wine.

SOURDOUGH TOAST WITH RAW TAHINI & DATE SYRUP

THIS ONE IS LESS OF A RECIPE AND MORE OF A SERVING SUGGESTION. RAW WHOLE TAHINI IS REALLY DELICIOUS WHEN SPREAD DIRECTLY FROM THE JAR OVER TOASTED SLICES OF SOURDOUGH BREAD. SIMPLY DRIZZLE WITH SOME DATE SYRUP AND DEVOUR. IT MIGHT SEEM A LITTLE "HARDCORE" FOR THOSE NOT BROUGHT UP ON THE TASTE OF TAHINI, BUT EVERYONE WE'VE EVER SERVED THIS TO HAS LOVED IT.

154

FREE-FROM LIST	GLUTEN–FREE	LACTOSE–FREE	NUT–FREE
Hummus Recipe	✓	✓	✓

TOPPINGS

	GLUTEN–FREE	LACTOSE–FREE	NUT–FREE
Hummus with Slow-cooked Chickpeas	✓	✓	✓
Hummus with Mushrooms	✓	✓	✓
Hummus with Chicken	✓	✓	✓
Hummus with Chunky Beef	✓	✓	✓
Hummus with Lamb & Pine Nuts	✓	✗	✗
Hummus with Lamb Rogan Josh	✓	✗	✓
Hummus with Chili con Carne	✓	✓	✓
Hummus with Mexican Beef	✓	✗	✓
Hummus with Moroccan Meatballs	✗	✓	✓
Masabacha	✓	✓	✓
Hummus with Fava Beans	✓	✓	✓
Shakshuka	✓	✓	✓
Hummus with Spicy Sausage & Three-Pepper Stew	✓	✓	✓
Hummus with Chicken Tikka Masala	✓	✗	✗

FALAFEL

	GLUTEN–FREE	LACTOSE–FREE	NUT–FREE
Green Falafel	✓	✓	✓
Sweet Potato Falafel	✓	✓	✓
Spicy Red Falafel	✓	✓	✓
Mixed Bean Falafel	✓	✓	✓

WRAPS

	GLUTEN–FREE	LACTOSE–FREE	NUT–FREE
Falafel Wrap	✗	✗	✓
Sabich: Eggplant & Egg Wrap	✗	✓	✓
Beef Wrap	✗	✓	✓

SOUPS

	GLUTEN–FREE	LACTOSE–FREE	NUT–FREE
Chickpea & Chorizo Soup	✓	✓	✓
Tomato Soup with Pita Bread Croutons	✗	✓	✓
Tomato Soup without Pita Bread Croutons	✓	✓	✓
Spicy Lentil Soup	✓	✓	✓
Mixed Bean & Bacon Soup	✗	✓	✓
Jerusalem Artichoke Soup with Chestnut Cream	✓	✗	✗

SALADS

	GLUTEN–FREE	LACTOSE–FREE	NUT–FREE
Roasted Eggplant Salad	✓	✓	✓
Roasted Vegetable Salad	✓	✓	✓

	GLUTEN-FREE	LACTOSE-FREE	NUT-FREE	155
Tabouleh	✗	✓	✓	
Mixed Vegetable Salad	✓	✓	✓	
Falafel Salad	✓	✗	✓	
Greek Salad	✓	✗	✓	
Fatoush	✗	✓	✓	
Cauliflower with Green Tahini	✓	✓	✓	

BREADS AND SAUCES

	GLUTEN-FREE	LACTOSE-FREE	NUT-FREE
Tahini Sauce	✓	✓	✓
Green Tahini Sauce	✓	✓	✓
Guacamole	✓	✓	✓
Tzatziki	✓	✗	✓
Tomato & Cilantro Salsa	✓	✓	✓
Green Chili Sauce	✓	✓	✓
Yellow Sauce	✓	✓	✓
Garlic & Lemon Sauce	✓	✓	✓
Whole Wheat Pita Bread	✗	✓	✓
Flatbread with Za'atar	✗	✓	✓
Labaneh (Sour Yogurt Cheese)	✓	✗	✓

DESSERTS

	GLUTEN-FREE	LACTOSE-FREE	NUT-FREE
Malabi	✓	✗	✓
Chocolate Brownies	✓	✗	✓
Halvah Parfait	✓	✗	✓
Orange Blossom Rice Pudding	✓	✗	✓
Panna Cotta with Rose Water	✓	✗	✓

DRINKS

	GLUTEN-FREE	LACTOSE-FREE	NUT-FREE
Mint & Ginger Lemonade	✓	✓	✓
Hot Spiced Apple Cider	✓	✓	✓
Cardamom Coffee	✓	✓	✓
Mint & Sage Teas	✓	✓	✓
Sachlav	✓	✗	✗
Ouzo & Grapefruit Slush	✓	✓	✓

QUICK SNACKS

	GLUTEN-FREE	LACTOSE-FREE	NUT-FREE
Halvah Cookies	✗	✗	✓
Morning Granola	✗	✓ (unless served with milk or yogurt)	✗
Salt-Pickled Cucumbers	✓	✓	✓
Pickled Lemons	✓	✓	✓
Spiced Fava Bean Nibbles	✓	✓	✓

ACKNOWLEDGMENTS

HUMMUS BROS. WOULD NOT BE WITHOUT THE SUPPORT AND DEDICATION OF THE FOLLOWING PEOPLE.

Noam Givon, who has been with us from Day One. Artur Kaczmarczyk, for making all the wonderful food we serve each day. Fred Edwards, who believed in us from the first meeting. Varun Khanna, our unofficial chairman emeritus, for putting his money where his mouth is. Ivo Slezak and Artur Karasiewicz, for sticking with us and giving 100%. Ryan Matzner, our original marketing genius, and Eran Hovav, who helped set everything up at first.

Arik, Roy Glanfield, and Carl Smith, for always supplying us with the best ingredients. Tim Chakera and Philip Otvos, whose work and opinions have been invaluable for the last nine years.

Roly Grant and Phil Koh at Buro Creative, for helping us convince our customers. Martin Chamberlain and Benjamin Davis, for supporting our initial growth.

Thank you to Karen Thomas for the beautiful photos, Sara Lewis for home economy, food styling (and importantly for developing the recipes to be suitable for home cooks!), Wei Tang for props, Laura Russell and Emma Wicks for book design, Kathy Steer for the copy editing, Kom Patel for marketing, and Simon Ballard for our portrait picture. A special thanks to Emily Preece-Morrison for producing this book from start to finish.

Thanks to George Grylls for being such a loyal fan and helping this book happen.

Thank you to Hannah and Orat for ten years of developing and testing recipes.

Finally, we'd like to dedicate this book to our families who have encouraged us every step of the way.

Christian Mouysset & Ronen Givon
The Hummus Brothers

Branch locations in the UK
Soho: 88 Wardour Street, London W1F 0TJ
Holborn: Victoria House, 37-63 Southampton Row, London WC1B 4DA
St Paul's: 128 Cheapside, London EC2V 6BT
Exmouth Market: 62 Exmouth Market, London EC1R 4QE

For more information, visit:
www.hbros.co.uk
facebook.com/hbros
twitter.com/hbros

METRO BOOKS
New York
An imprint of Sterling Publishing
1166 Avenue of the Americas,
17th floor
New York, NY 10036

METRO BOOKS and the distinctive Metro Books logo are trademarks of
Sterling Publishing Co., Inc.

Commissioning editor: Emily Preece-Morrison
Design and layout: Laura Russell and Emma Wicks
Home economist and recipe developer: Sara Lewis
Photographer: Karen Thomas, except image on p. 7 by Simon Ballard
Stylist: Wei Tang
Copy editor: Kathy Steer
Indexer: Ruth Ellis
Americanizer: Theresa Bebbington

Home economist and recipe developer: Sara Lewis
Photographer: Karen Thomas, except image on p.7 by Simon Ballard

ISBN 978-1-4351-5480-3 (Hardback)

For information about custom editions, special sales, and premium and corporate purchases,
please contact Sterling Special Sales at 800-805-5489 or specialsales@sterlingpublishing.com.

Manufactured in China

2 4 6 8 10 9 7 5 3 1

www.sterlingpublishing.com